The Ministry *of* Lament

To my parents

*I am dedicating this book to my mother, Mary Lenna Fowler,
who succumbed to Alzheimer's disease in October 2008,
and to my father, Gene T. Fowler, Sr.,
who cared for my mother lovingly and faithfully
throughout her illness.*

The Ministry *of* Lament
Caring *for the* Bereaved

GENE FOWLER

CHALICE
PRESS

ST. LOUIS, MISSOURI

Cover image: FotoSearch
Cover and interior design: Elizabeth Wright

Visit Chalice Press on the World Wide Web at
www.chalicepress.com

10 9 8 7 6 5 4 3 2 1   10 11 12 13 14 15

EPDF: 978-08272-23516   EPUB: 978-08272-23509

Library of Congress Cataloging–in–Publication Data

Fowler, Gene, 1952-
The ministry of lament : caring for the bereaved / by Gene Fowler.
    p. cm.
Includes bibliographical references.
ISBN 978-0-8272-2335-6
1. Church work with the bereaved. 2. Pastoral theology. 3. Bereavement—Religious aspects—Christianity. I. Title.
BV4330.F695 2010
259'.6—dc22

2009047111

Printed in the United States of America

Contents

Acknowledgments

It is common to see an editor acknowledged in this section of a book, but I want to acknowledge Publisher and President of Chalice Press Cyrus N. White. I was delayed in finishing this book for several months due to circumstances beyond my control. He showed uncommon patience and care during this time, and he deserves much thanks. I also want to thank my wife, Amy, for her love and patience and for her feedback on some chapters of the book. Finally, I want to thank my good friend Rev. Curtis Page for his wisdom about pastoral ministry and for his insights on an early draft of a chapter in the book.

Introduction

Writing about bereavement is humbling. Grief seeps into many hidden crevices of human life, and its impact on real people goes beyond what concepts and metaphors have the power to convey. Nor can the actual pastoral care of those who care for bereaved people in congregations be adequately captured and contained in writing. Pastors and those who participate in congregations go through much more in their ministry of caring for the bereaved than books can portray. Yet caring for grieving people in the congregational setting still deserves serious attention in writing, whatever the inherent limitations of the endeavor.

Caring for grieving people in congregations extends all the way from the occasional private pastoral counseling conversation to grief support groups to the caring potential found in the communal life of the congregation, including its religious practices. In light of the broad spectrum of caring possibilities in congregations, my thesis is that understanding the relationship between spirituality and bereavement is essential for practicing the ministry of caring for those who grieve and mourn effectively. The book is about this relationship, including its implications for caring ministry in congregations.

Originally, the idea for this book emerged when I was writing about the beginning of grief and mourning in relation to funerals in *Caring Through the Funeral: A Pastor's Guide*. That book was about the church's short-term care of the bereaved from the beginning of the death through the funeral and a short time after it. I did not address the ministry of caring for the bereaved for the long term. The present book, however, goes through the entirety of bereavement seen in relation to the spiritual life of grieving people in the congregational setting.

For addressing spirituality and bereavement, I will draw on two main resources. In my funeral book, I drew on psychotherapist Therese Rando for understanding grief and mourning. One reason I found her work helpful was that she took the beginning of grief and mourning more seriously than most grief authors. In this book, I will continue drawing on Rando for the psychological understanding of grief and mourning from the beginning of bereavement throughout the long journey of grief and mourning. I also will draw on other contemporary psychotherapeutic authors in conjunction with Rando, but her schema of the mourning processes will provide the main organization of the discussion of grief and mourning throughout this book.

For discussing spirituality, I will draw on the psalms of lament in the book of Psalms because they address the relationship of a troubled person or community with God. Often, the lament psalms are used for discussing expressions of suffering, as if that were the only point of these psalms. They are far more than this. The lament psalms are poetry in which a suffering person is praying to God. This prayer exhibits an astounding array of imagery showing that the relationship with God has diverse and complex features. The lament psalms show the heights as well as the depths of the spiritual life. The biblical scholarship of Bernhard Anderson, as well as that of other Psalms commentators, will guide discussion of the lament psalms throughout the book. When I was writing the funeral book, I was fully aware of the lament psalms having been used for writing about pastoral counseling in grief situations in *Biblical Approaches to Pastoral Counseling* by pastoral theologian Donald Capps. In light of that book, I began thinking about the lament psalms being brought into dialogue with the mourning schema of Rando for exploring spirituality and bereavement in the long-term ministry of caring for bereaved people in the congregational setting. I want to give Capps full credit for being ahead of the game regarding the use of the lament psalms in caring ministry.

My use of the lament psalms explains the title of this book, *The Ministry of Lament: Caring for the Bereaved.* I am calling the ministry of caring for the bereaved in the congregational setting, the ministry of lament. Because the setting is the congregation, the book is intended primarily for pastors and lay leaders. Certainly, however, the ministry of caring for bereaved people exists in settings outside Christian congregations, such as in other religious traditions, chaplaincy, pastoral psychotherapy, psychiatry, clinical psychology, family therapy, and social work. The discussion of spirituality and bereavement can be applied in these settings, and I invite anyone who deals with grieving people to make use of this book, tailoring it to your setting and needs.

Chapter 1 will introduce the ministry of lament. The chapter includes a critique of the traditional pastoral care and counseling approach to grieving people. I will emphasize the caring potential of the congregation's communal life for the ministry of lament.

Chapter 2 is an introduction to bereavement and the main psychological and biblical resources to be used in the rest of the book. The chapter ends with a brief outline showing how the two resources will be brought into dialogue for developing an understanding of spirituality and bereavement.

In chapter 3, the discussion of spirituality and bereavement begins with the presentation of the first mourning process and the first part of the lament psalms. Next, the chapter will show how they are related in the life of a newly bereaved person. The chapter ends with implications for the ministry of lament.

Chapters 4 through 8 follow this same procedure. Each chapter presents a mourning process and the corresponding part of the lament psalms. Next, the two will be related in the context of focusing on bereaved people. Each chapter ends with implications for the ministry of lament.

You will find it helpful to keep one thing in mind while reading chapters 3 through 8. Traditionally, many psychotherapists have conceived of grief as a series of universal stages unfolding according to someone's preconceived timetable. That understanding of grief is no longer tenable. The ebb and flow of grief and mourning is far more diverse and dependent on the people involved, as well as the type of death and the circumstances surrounding it. Grief is more like taking the winding back roads than the dull, straight interstate when going somewhere. The chapters are not intended to be like the interstate, in which you start with the first mourning process and proceed step by step to the last one, knowing pretty closely when you should arrive at your destination. Instead, each chapter should be more like part of the winding road, in which you may get behind schedule, but you see some new territory. It may not matter that you get lost for a time and have to find your way again.

In this way, contemporary grief and mourning are more compatible with the spiritual life. As the poetry in the biblical lament psalms shows, the relationship of suffering people to God takes many twists and turns. For example, the psalmists frequently blame God for what is wrong. Observers, ministers, and friends have no reason and no right to place a time limit on this behavior. When the psalmist moves from this complaint to an expression of trusting in God's reliability, it is not a scheduled move in which the attitude of the suffering person toward God can just change on cue. The movement in the lament psalms reflects the winding road, not the interstate.

Finally, bereaved people will be portrayed as contemporary psalmists of lament. In many instances, their stories of mourning are explicit, but they contain spirituality inherently. I have used a variety of resources to tell these stories, including autobiographical books, psychiatric cases, movies, and church situations. The many ways that people share with others their mourning and their spiritual life demonstrate that ultimately we all are psalmists of lament. The relationship between spirituality and bereavement is within our own life stories, and we all have the potential to participate in the ministry of caring for others who grieve and mourn.

Pastoral Care as the Ministry of Lament

Many twenty-first-century pastors and congregations face an incredible challenge caring for huge numbers of grieving people in their churches. This chapter presents an understanding of pastoral care that can help pastors, church leaders, and congregations care for the bereaved over months and years. This understanding of caring for the bereaved is called the ministry of lament in accord with the psalms of lament used throughout the book.

A Pastor's Dilemma

Ten months after I became interim pastor of a congregation, I experienced something new in worship when the church celebrated All Saints Day in November, just preceding Thanksgiving and Advent. On the church calendar, All Saints Day normally appears during the week, but Protestant congregations often ignore it, as I had done in the past. This congregation, however, had been celebrating it for several years on the Sunday closest to the date. The ceremony was simple, but it gave me quite a lesson.

At the appointed time in the worship service, the name of every church member who died during the previous year was read. Following each name, a member of the hand bell choir rang a bell. Because six church members had died that year, six names were read, and the bell tolled six times. After the last name, the worshipers were invited to call out names from outside the congregation. These names could include any deceased person the worshiper wanted to remember, such as a family member, a friend, or a colleague from work who had died during the year. A name would be called and the bell rung.

I had expected a few names to be called, but I heard more than a few, many more. The naming and bell ringing seemed to go on and on. I did not count the number, nor did I look at my watch. At least twenty to thirty names were spoken in about fifteen minutes that seemed like thirty. A prayer ended this portion of the worship service, though the music, the sermon, and Holy Communion all fit the theme of All Saints Day.

This new and surprising experience opened my eyes to the breadth of bereavement in the congregation. Bereavement was far more widespread and prevalent than I, or anyone in the church, ever could have known before that day, because many were grieving deaths of people not associated with the congregation. An incredible amount of mourning lurked beneath the surface of the congregational community, waiting for a chance to emerge and be expressed through the voicing of names and the tolling of a bell.

This revelation presented a dilemma. How could I, or a group of trained lay caregivers for that matter, possibly respond to every grieving person in the traditional sense of having timely pastoral care and counseling conversation through the course of the grief process? For the sake of argument, let's say that thirty-one names were called out in the All Saints Day ceremony. Others called out no name but were in their second year of bereavement. We could go on to the third year and beyond, and the number would keep going up, for grief is no respecter of time. Others were experiencing different kinds of loss whose reaction involves grief, such as divorce and job loss. And this is just one relatively small congregation!

The idea of pastors and clinically trained lay caregivers having weekly pastoral care and counseling conversation month after month with the dozens upon dozens of bereaved people populating many congregations is an unrealistic notion. Consequently, the traditional view of pastoral care and counseling is not sufficient in this case.

This view will be even less effective in the future with the aging of the large Baby Boomer generation. Churches will fill increasingly with aging adults, adult children, and grandchildren who mourn the loss of their boomer friends, parents, and grandparents. Church leaders must create another means of caring, or the ministry of caring for the bereaved is hopeless.

Something More Is Needed

It would be quite helpful if churches saw the All Saints Day worship service itself as a way of caring for the bereaved. But in the traditional understanding of pastoral care and counseling just mentioned, still prevalent in most churches, the worship service I discussed above would not be seen as a way of caring for the bereaved normally, no matter how meaningful it may have been to grieving worshipers as they approached the holidays. Instead, the worship service would tend to be seen as an occasion presenting the possibility of future private counseling conversation with some worshipers whose bereavement was revealed because they called out a name. Even if people saw this special worship service as a way of caring for the bereaved, it would be practiced only once a year, consequently having only limited use. Clearly, something more is needed.

Think about what actually happens in churches regarding care of bereaved people. First, comes the funeral. Naturally, private conversation happens before the funeral, but all such conversation ultimately is geared toward the funeral, the most important means of caring for the bereaved during the first part of grieving. The Christian funeral is a worship service, not private counseling.

Next come the first few days and weeks following the funeral. During this time, the pastor may visit the grieving person or family. This pastoral visit is a ritual of the church in which the pastor and grieving church member, or members, reconnect post-funeral. In this reconnection, the pastor shows acceptance of the bereaved person or persons as church members who are grieving.

The next part of reconnection comes when the bereaved person or family returns to worship following the funeral. This shows that the congregation as a whole accepts grieving people as part of the congregational community and that the bereaved are indeed reestablishing relationships with their religious community, though this reconnection may be fragile depending on circumstances.

Of course, a bereaved person or family may return to church before a pastoral visit happens, but the main point is that the bereaved reconnect both with the pastor and congregation. The church could not exist if bereavement were not an accepted part of the congregation, because a significant percentage of the people who comprise the congregation have known grief, do know grief, and are not strangers to the bereavement of others. The word *acceptance* cannot be taken in an infantile all-or-nothing way, however, as if the congregation were a community whose participants exuded some superhuman perfection.

As weeks and months pass, the most common scenario is that bereaved people resume their participation in the congregation. By this time, ongoing pastoral care and counseling of the bereaved can seem to have disappeared almost completely. Yes, someone may send cards at anniversary times, or the church may offer the occasional grief group. Those grieving may receive some visitation or a counseling conversation now and then, but overall in the life of the church an intentional pastoral care and counseling focus on the bereaved person ends as new deaths occur and as pastors make decisions about how time is to be spent. This is where something more really is needed.

Do Congregations Abandon the Bereaved?

If pastors and trained lay caregivers are supposed to be having weekly, or near weekly, pastoral care and counseling conversations with grieving people month after month, the church is failing in this task. Pastoral theologian Allan Cole writes that ministers and faith communities do a credible job caring for the bereaved up to a week following the death. But after this their efforts fall short: "Ministers and faith communities usually intend to provide adequate longer-term care and support, but typically their efforts fall short. They neglect the needs of the bereaved" (2008, 61). It is unfair to say that ministers and faith communities can sustain good care of the bereaved only for a week. But one cannot deny the view that longer-term care typically falls short, assuming that this care is supposed to involve pastoral care and counseling conversation in ongoing pastoral visitation.

So what is the problem? Are ministers and faith communities uncaring or lazy? No. The problem is that the pastoral care and counseling view of caring for the bereaved in the congregational setting is unrealistic in the sense that it is unworkable, with hardly any exceptions. In the mid-twentieth century, the pastoral care and counseling movement created the ideal that following the funeral ministers should care for bereaved individuals by visiting them month after month, weekly at first and then lengthening the time between visits, having a counseling conversation during each visit. In the 1950s, even funerals were seen as a way of preparing bereaved family members for counseling with the pastor as the means of pastoral care during the months following the funeral (see Paul Irion, *The Funeral and the Mourners*, 1954, 159).

In 1974, pastoral theologian David Switzer laid out what he called a schedule for grief counseling. After pre-funeral pastoral visits with the family of the deceased, the funeral, and a follow-up visit, the minister was to begin weekly pastoral care and counseling conversations with the bereaved church member:

There should be continued regular pastoral conversations, approximately weekly during the first six weeks and then moving to perhaps every ten days to two weeks for another six weeks or so, and then tapering off into less frequent contacts as grief work seems to be in the process of being accomplished, the pain diminishing somewhat, and activities and relationships being renewed. (1974, 157–58)

More recently, in 2000, Switzer reaffirmed this view in an updated chapter, extending the time frame for weekly visits from six weeks to two or three months. He writes:

Pastoral concern needs to be offered to the grief-stricken persons for considerably longer than a single post-funeral call within a week after the service. In some parishes, it may be possible for the one ordained person to visit on a weekly basis over a period of two or three months, then every two or three weeks for another several months. Probably not every bereaved person needs such an amount or extent of time, but some number do. (2000, 114)

He then allows for variations in larger congregations: "Of course, there are many congregations and communities where the clergy really don't have that much time. In some cases, other persons on the church staff or trained laypersons might be able to carry on this type of pastoral care" (2000, 114).

As Switzer indicates, the pastoral care and counseling ideal for the ministry of caring for the bereaved remains in force to this day in pastoral theology, and it continues to inform ministers and faith communities. Unfortunately, however, it is not workable as far as actual ministry in congregations is concerned, whatever the size of the congregation. This counseling ideal lacks viability for twenty-first–century pastors and congregations for the several reasons. First, many congregations have large numbers of bereaved people. Consequently, weekly and near weekly pastoral visitation for months on end with the bereaved in these congregations is not feasible.

Second, time management constraints in pastoral ministry are real and do not allow for the scheduling of visitation prescribed in the pastoral care and counseling model. They are real in small church solo pastorates, which are the vast majority, and they are real in the minority of larger multi-staff congregations. Ministers must balance their schedule so they can accomplish their various weekly duties in accord with congregational expectations. If this alone were taken seriously, it would be enough to call into question the pastoral care and counseling view of post-funeral care.

Another time management issue is even more significant. The nature of pastoral ministry requires a flexible weekly schedule. In any given week circumstances arising unexpectedly may require daily revision of a pastor's schedule. For instance, a church member's emergency operation on Tuesday may be followed by another church member's death on Thursday. If the pastor had allotted just enough sermon-writing time, now the sermon preparation must be pushed back; and appointments must be cancelled or rescheduled. The following week's schedule, too, must be revised to make room for the funeral and its preparation. This may require more cancellations and rescheduling and pushing back of sermon preparation. And so it goes. The point is not that a pastoral visit must sometimes get rescheduled. Rather, the notion of the pastor having multiple weekly visits with the bereaved, which could take up at least half the workweek or more in many congregations, flies in the face of reality in pastoral ministry.

Third, the extensive pastoral visitation in the homes of church members that this caring method requires is simply unreal in the twenty-first century. Since World War II, pastoral ministry has been adjusting to changing societal patterns of living, in which dropping in on neighbors and friends has, for all practical purposes, gone away for the most part. In today's world, pastors are not making regular visits in church members' homes according to their own schedules, as if making chaplain-like rounds in a hospital—for one thing, most would not be home because so many work during the day or have otherwise busy lives, including retirees. Normally, pastors must phone church members to schedule an appointment days or weeks in advance, and even this can be complicated. Consider the example of a woman who lost her husband to a tragic car wreck and now is the single parent of two toddlers. Unless this person is an executive, she may get in trouble at work for taking a personal phone call. In this case, the pastor must phone at night, when the person is preparing dinner for the kids, getting them ready for bed, or finally collapsing after a long day. Because the person works, the pastoral visit would have to take place in the evening. Like most church members, this young widow never has experienced pastoral visits in the home, so anxiety is raised. The house must be cleaned up, refreshments prepared, and someone must be available to care for the kids. If she is offered the option of coming to the pastor's office, this is the option she will choose inevitably. But this option also has its set of complications. Because the appointment must be in the evening, she must hire a babysitter, but that costs money. Finally, if the pastor is male, meeting with the widow regularly at night either in her home or the office could lead to gossip, so another adult needs to be in the home or in the church when they meet. This is not conducive to meeting weekly for months. Many scenarios are possible, but hardly any are conducive to weekly pastoral visitation. Bereaved people work, raise families, become exhausted at night, have medical appointments, and generally lead busy lives like others. Moreover, if they believe they need weekly counseling, they will likely see a psychotherapist. Many church members have been to therapy at some point in their lives, and they do not want their pastor to be a therapist.

Fourth, pastors should not practice long-term pastoral counseling, lasting for months and potentially over a year, with any church member. If a pastor feels that a grieving church member needs weekly counseling conversation for months, referral to a therapist is appropriate.

Fifth, the mid-twentieth–century psychological models of grief, such as grief seen as a series of stages, are being seriously questioned today and even rejected. Consequently, twenty-first–century pastors and congregations should not be saddled with a mid-twentieth–century understanding of care and counseling based on outdated models of grief. For instance, contemporary psychological models of grief do not support a yearlong time frame for grief, in the recognition that grief does not unfold on a preconceived schedule within a certain time period viewed as nearly the same for everyone. Consequently, twenty-first–century ministers and faith communities should not be confined to a pastoral care and counseling plan designed only for several months, up to a year or so.

I want to be clear that I am not arguing against pastoral care and counseling in general. Instead, I am concerned about a specific mid-twentieth–century understanding of caring for the bereaved that still influences ministers and faith communities. I have tried to show that this understanding is problematic. It has been a setup in which ministers and faith communities have been criticized unfairly for decades, because they have not been able to put the model into practice.

Neither ministers nor faith communities should feel guilty about not living up to the unworkable ideal of twentieth-century pastoral care and counseling in the realm of caring for the bereaved. Yet pastoral theologians, ministers, and faith communities all share a certain responsibility for this situation. This responsibility is at the level of the relationship between the church and society.

Church and Society

During the twentieth century, American society began supporting a way for people to address their grief on a regular basis for months and years, namely, psychotherapy. In the twenty-first century, psychotherapy has long since become the primary setting in which Americans are encouraged to address their grief and its painful feelings, as well as other forms of suffering. The church participates in this through pastoral care and counseling.

The workplace provides a telling example. On the one hand, the need for time and space to grieve runs headlong into business. To keep from being fired, a grieving person must produce at work rather than taking needed time off. On the other hand, many companies provide medical benefits that include payment for seeing a psychotherapist. Yet many citizens do not have medical coverage, making this an ongoing social issue involving humanitarian, medical, political, economic, and religious aspects. Both society and the church seem to have the same problem—not being able to provide psychotherapeutic help to all the bereaved. This view, however, presumes the desire of every bereaved person to receive psychotherapeutic help, though nothing could be further from the truth.

As a result of its commitment to psychotherapy, society has moved away from supporting more public means of addressing grief. It makes sense that public expressions of grief and mourning are discouraged, because maintaining confidentiality about what is said in a therapy session is one hallmark of psychotherapy. The psychotherapist does not tell what is discussed in a therapy session, nor are individuals expected to disclose what they discuss in therapy. It would be rude to ask. This value of confidentiality has impacted the church, seen in scholarly criticisms of the church for avoiding public expressions of suffering, such as avoiding the use of the lament psalms in worship. But this is a double bind. If the church encourages public expressions of suffering, it goes against the main societal orientation of caring for the bereaved in private settings, in which pastors are trained to participate. Yet if the church supports the practice of pastoral care and counseling of the bereaved, safeguarding confidentiality, it opens itself to criticism for abandoning the public forms of grieving.

A good example of the rise of psychotherapy for addressing grief is the famous mid-twentieth–century article by psychiatrist Eric Lindemann entitled, "Symptomotology and Management of Acute Grief." According to Lindemann, "The essential task facing the psychiatrist is that of sharing the patient's work—namely, his efforts at extricating himself from the bondage to the deceased and at finding new patterns of rewarding interaction" (1944/1979, 74).

In this mid-twentieth–century view, developed during World War II, grief was seen as a medical difficulty, implicitly putting it in the realm of disease from which the bereaved individual needed to be healed. The grieving person became a patient, the psychiatrist was the expert doctor who treated the patient, and grief work was the vehicle driving the psychotherapeutic process to completion. This is why Lindemann could use words such as "extricating" and "bondage," as if grief were a horrible illness needing a cure as soon as possible.

Though this older medical framework for understanding grief may not be current, Lindemann's phrase, "grief work," became a staple in the psychiatric grief lexicon. Likewise, contemporary approaches to grieving and mourning are connected to psychotherapy every bit as much as during the mid-twentieth century. Accordingly, in the United States today, bereaved people are seen as potential patients or clients who need the expert, the psychotherapist, for working through their grief; and the church continues participating in this view through pastoral care and counseling.

I want to be clear here also, that I am not arguing against psychotherapy or psychological understandings of grief. In the rest of the book, I will make extensive use of psychology. Nor am I arguing that the church should not participate in contemporary, socially supported means of healing. Rather, the particular way that pastoral theologians, ministers, and faith communities have been participating in this is not working and needs to change, which requires focusing on the religious side of the ledger.

The Church and Psychiatry

Lindemann, in his World War II article cited above, recognized that psychiatrists alone could not handle the massive number of bereaved people—quite an understatement. He suggested that "auxiliary workers" would be needed, specifically social workers and ministers: "Social workers and ministers will have to be on the lookout for the more ominous pictures, referring these to the psychiatrist while assisting the more normal reactions themselves." This, of course, required that ministers and social workers learn psychotherapeutic method, supplementing the psychotherapeutic effort of the psychiatrist (1979, 76).

That pastors have ever seen themselves as "auxiliary workers" for psychiatrists, even in the realm of caring for the bereaved, is highly doubtful. What church member proudly introduces their pastor as an "auxiliary worker" in mental health? Yet suggestions like this one of Lindemann fit perfectly with developments happening in pastoral care education during the mid-twentieth century. Seminary students were participating in new clinical training programs found primarily in medical centers, in what today is called Clinical Pastoral Education, with its historic psychotherapeutic emphasis. Following World War II, the church increasingly embraced psychotherapy, as future pastors began learning psychotherapeutic methods in new pastoral care and counseling courses in seminaries and divinity schools. In the 1960s, the American Association of Pastoral Counselors was born, enabling clergy to become full-time pastoral counseling specialists.

These new pastoral care developments made it possible to appropriate what Lindemann wrote about the church in his article, in which he compared the church to psychotherapy. He wrote that the main way churches, or what he called religious agencies, have cared for grieving people historically is by providing comfort. Though he failed to define comfort, he did give illustrations: "They have provided comfort by giving the backing of dogma to the patient's wish for continued interaction with the deceased, have developed rituals that maintain the patient's interaction with others, and have counteracted the morbid guilt feelings of the patient by Divine Grace and by promising an opportunity for 'making up' to the deceased at the time of a later reunion." Lindemann did acknowledge that these religious means of comfort had helped countless mourners. But he judged that this help was still inadequate: "comfort alone does not provide adequate assistance in the patient's grief work." Instead, the "adequate assistance" came from psychotherapy. Amazingly, Lindemann contended that the many grief work tasks to be accomplished in psychotherapy could be done in eight to ten sessions (1979, 74–75).

Using psychotherapy methods in pastoral care and counseling is still conceived as the predominant way that churches should care for the bereaved. Consequently, even today the church implicitly shares with Lindemann the assumption that psychotherapy provides more "adequate assistance" to grieving people than "Divine Grace" or any of the church's other beliefs and practices.

A Destructive Split

One way this implicit assumption can play out in a congregation is that pastors and church members split off their understanding of pastoral care and counseling from their religious practices. On one side of the split, pastoral care and counseling is the private counseling conversation involving the pastor or a trained lay caregiver and a church member, couple, or family. The traditional view that pastoral counseling has an implicit theological dimension does not negate this split. Nor does it matter that pastoral care and counseling can include the use of religious resources, such as prayer and scripture. They always have been included as one kind of therapeutic resource among others within the context of a pastoral counseling conversation.

On the other side of the split are the explicitly religious practices of the Christian faith, in which people bring the issues of their lives before God in worship, prayer, and so forth. But this is not conceived as having anything to do with official pastoral care and counseling, even if one assumes that the communal religious life of the congregation is helpful in some way. It is as if two unrelated systems of care are going on simultaneously: official pastoral care and counseling, and unofficial religious practices in the communal life of the congregation. The All Saints Day worship service I discussed at the beginning of the chapter is a case in point.

Some lines from a contemporary psalm of lament by Ann Weems reflect this split beautifully:

> In my suffering
> I am told I must
> grieve correctly.
> O merciful God!
> What are they doing?
> Aren't we supposed
> to go to you with our tears? (1994, 22)

Healing the Split and Becoming a Caring Church

The continuing assumption of the church favoring psychotherapeutic methods over the Christian faith in caring for bereaved people must be abandoned. This does not mean simply switching assumptions and favoring religious practices over psychotherapeutic methods. It is not a matter of declaring one means of care superior to another.

Instead, the church should step out of the competition altogether in its care of the bereaved. Lindemann made a foil of religion to lift up his own advances in psychotherapy with grieving people. Apparently, advances often require a foil, or a straw dog to knock down. However, neither the Christian faith nor other faith traditions should be a foil for psychotherapy, just as psychotherapy should not be a foil for the church. Stepping out of the competition gives the pastor and congregation a new freedom to heal the split between pastoral care and counseling and the rest of congregational life as it relates to bereavement.

The Ministry of Lament: Healing the Split

In the ministry of lament, pastors and church members affirm that the entire communal life of the congregation contains caring potential. This affirmation forms the first step in healing the split. In this affirmation, the communal life of the church includes ordinary weekly worship, prayer, small groups focused on spiritual growth, biblical study, fellowship, and even the various outreach ministries of the congregation, such as mission projects and evangelism. The congregation's ministry of caring for grieving people first and foremost involves leading with its strength by being a faithful religious community with its ceremonies, groups, fellowship, prayers, and ministries.

Ongoing pastoral care and counseling conversation cannot sustain the long-term care of the bereaved. Yet having such conversation on an occasional basis definitely is part of the church's life, along with the other things just mentioned. In the ministry of lament, pastoral care and counseling conversation exists as a relatively modest part of a much larger caring ministry involving the entire communal life of the congregation.

Naming the Congregation's Caring Potential

If a pastor and congregation can acknowledge that the communal life of the congregation has caring potential and is part of the caring ministry, they can take the next step toward healing the split. This involves realizing that one important aspect of grieving involves the bereaved person's spirituality, which, according to sociologist of religion Robert Wuthnow, "is the shorthand term we use in our society to talk about a person's relationship with God." In the ministry of lament, the pastor and congregation attend to the bereaved person's relationship with God. As Wuthnow says, "For many people, how they think about it is certainly guided by what they see and do in their congregations" (2007, 112).

Within the context of this focus, all life in the church is viewed as having an influence on the grieving person's bereavement, because participation in the faith community influences the grieving person's relationship with God. This is why the ministry of lament includes the affirmation that the communal life of the church has caring potential. Clearly, this affirmation is no substitution of communal religious practices for psychotherapy. Rather, it is practicing the Christian faith for an explicitly spiritual purpose. Nor is it an argument against pastoral care and counseling. Rather, the ministry of lament relates the life of the church to bereaved people who maintain a spiritual life in the context of the faith community. Therefore, those who plan and participate in the communal practices of the church should do so with a growing attunement to every facet of bereavement, including grief understood psychologically.

Grieving people who participate in the life of the church should be enabled to address their relationship to God fruitfully, over time, in ways that are meaningful with respect to their ongoing journey of grief. This does not mean other parts of a bereaved person's life are not of concern, for all aspects of a person's life are included in this spiritual relationship inherently. Attending to a person's relationship with God is virtually a doorway into the whole of an individual's life.

Those who grieve do bring bereavement into their relationship with God. Grief influences their spiritual journey, sometimes dramatically and sometimes more subtly. This does not mean that grief always should be the center of concern in a bereaved person's spiritual life over time. Rather, the ministry of lament acknowledges that grief does influence a bereaved person's spiritual life. Consequently, pastors and church members should strive to make the congregation a community where a grieving person can ask hard questions and where faith is not viewed superficially as a bed of roses.

Those who grieve cannot help but bring God into their grief. Many bereaved people turn to God for help. This reality needs to be taken seriously by each and every person who cares for grieving people. The church should affirm unabashedly that God does care and does help. The church should affirm that God not only comforts, as Lindemann indicated, but walks through the agonizing times with us. The church should affirm that God brings healing to the wounded soul and brings positive change into human lives.

Bereaved people also continue having a spiritual life over time, in the sense of maintaining a relationship with God throughout their grieving, though this relationship may have many fluctuations. For instance, bereaved people who attend worship on a regular basis are participating in a ceremony in which the divine and human relationship is addressed explicitly. This reality indicates that weekly worship necessarily affects the lives of those who have suffered loss. Every congregation should take into account the presence of grieving people in its planning and practice of worship, as well as other facets of church life.

God in Contemporary Pastoral Care and Counseling

Another part of the split needing healing involves the way the Christian faith is viewed in pastoral care and counseling today versus the way it is viewed in the rest of congregational life. Pastors and church members should not have to think of their religion one way in pastoral care and counseling and another way in the rest of their life in the congregation.

Without a doubt, contemporary pastoral care and counseling allows for talking about God explicitly and using religious resources. Pastoral theologian John Patton calls this the classical paradigm, whose primary feature is "the message of a God who caringly creates human beings for relationship and who continues to care by hearing and remembering them." It began, he says, with the advent of Christianity, continued through the Reformation, and ended as the main paradigm of care with "the advent of modern dynamic psychology's impact on ministry." He places this paradigm alongside a second one developed in the twentieth century, called the clinical pastoral paradigm, when psychotherapy was incorporated into care, and a third contemporary paradigm, called the communal contextual paradigm, in which the focus is on the contexts of care, and virtually all the social sciences begin playing a role in care (1993, 4–5).

More recently, pastoral theologian Carrie Doehring has developed a similar view, calling the paradigms premodern, modern, and postmodern. These are three interpretive lenses through which to view the pastoral care and counseling situation, in which the premodern lens corresponds most closely to Patton's classical paradigm. Doehring says that when using a premodern lens, "pastors assume for the moment that God or that which is sacred can be glimpsed and apprehended to some degree through sacred texts, religious rituals and traditions, and religious and spiritual experiences—the way transcendent realities seemed to be known within the ancient and medieval church" (2006, 2).

On the one hand, it is encouraging that historic religious approaches to the ministry of care are being incorporated into contemporary pastoral care and counseling, to go along with modern approaches that make use of psychology and with postmodern contextual approaches that make use of social sciences. On the other hand, the terms *classical* and *premodern* are unfortunate labels for the Christian message about God and explicit religious practices experienced in the ministry of care today. Inevitably, these labels carry the negative connotation that something premodern is not as good or helpful as something modern, such as psychotherapy, or postmodern, such as discerning ways that society and culture influence human ways of knowing. We saw this earlier in the Lindemann discussion.

Moreover, these two labels imply that all practice of the Christian faith, not just in times of care, ends up in a historical straightjacket. For instance, consider a statement by Doehring that could apply to someone who just learned that a loved one has died suddenly. She writes, "In the initial shock and denial of acute moments of crisis, people often function out of a premodern mode, appealing to God to intervene in their crisis." No inherent distinction exists between this appeal for divine intervention and, for example, a sermon, a prayer, or worship itself. Presumably, if, in a worship service, a pastor prays that a grieving family receive consolation from God, that pastor and the congregation are functioning "out of a premodern mode" (2006, 116).

Ultimately, the entire Christian religion comes to be seen only as a premodern institution, like an old church building seeming out of place now that it sits in the shadows of new skyscrapers built all around it. This is like saying that all medical practice is premodern or classical, because medicine existed centuries ago. Consequently, such care theories or models provide no accounting for the actual practice of the Christian faith in the modern era and now in the postmodern era, other than calling it premodern or classical. This shortchanges the Christian community, as well as other religious traditions. The religion of the community of faith exists in the present among contemporary generations of people and must be taken seriously as part of the present, not as a regression to a past way of knowing.

The ministry of lament, including pastoral care and counseling conversation, requires that the Christian faith as it exists in twenty-first–century congregations be considered on its own terms, as a contemporary reality in the world today. People who suffer the loss of loved ones are standing face-to-face with life and death, with meaning, and with an uncertain future. The last thing in the world any pastor or congregation needs is a divided understanding of the Christian faith, understood as part of the past in pastoral care and counseling and understood as contemporary in the rest of church life.

What Next?

The ministry of lament involves caring for bereaved people in the congregational setting. Traditional pastoral care and counseling conversation is part of this ministry, but only a part. Such pastoral conversation exists as an occasional practice within the context of the entire communal life of the congregation, all of which contains caring potential.

Affirming the caring potential of life together in the congregation is important because grieving people in the church have a relationship with God. This relationship is affected by grief, and, in turn, this relationship also affects the grief. Participation in the community of faith facilitates the ongoing development of this relationship to the divine in whatever ways are needed during the course of bereavement. Out of this participation the occasional pastoral counseling conversation may arise, grief support groups get organized, and ongoing supportive lay care happens, most often in informal ways. However, only through this participation over time is the church enabled to care for the many grieving people in its midst over long time periods, well beyond a few months or a year.

The question, then, is not whether pastors and congregations stop caring for the bereaved, but whether they are growing in their understanding of spirituality and grief, and reflecting this understanding in the ongoing life of the church, so that participation in the congregation can be increasingly meaningful for the bereaved. This is the primary concern in the rest of the book. The next chapter will present the resources to be used for this exploration.

CHAPTER 2

Introducing Mourning and Lament

To practice the ministry of lament, pastors and congregations need to learn more about ways bereaved people relate to God. To learn more about this, they can use resources that address bereavement and resources that address relating to God. This chapter will introduce psychological resources for understanding bereavement and the psalms of lament for understanding ways people in distress relate to God. I will discuss the psychological resources following an introduction to bereavement. Then I will introduce the psalms of lament. The chapter concludes with an outline showing how I will bring the two resources into dialogue beginning in chapter 3.

Bereavement

When I began exploring the words people use for naming the experience of losing someone to death, I quickly learned that the English language has no word addressing this one circumstance exclusively. Bereavement comes closest. Bereavement means finding yourself in the state of being deprived. Someone has been taken from you because that person has died. The deceased person can be a relative, a friend, or anyone with whom you have an endearing emotional connection, according to the *Oxford English Dictionary*. The dictionary also reveals that the ancient root of bereavement, *reave*, includes in its meaning forcibly taking a person away from this life or from earth to heaven. Historically even though a person can be deprived of many different things, bereavement has included being deprived of another person through death.

The key to understanding bereavement lies in the quality of deprivation a person experiences as a result of the death. Imagine you are walking down the street one evening and are about to get in your car parked nearby. Suddenly a stranger appears out of nowhere and robs you at gunpoint, taking all your money, your watch, your jewelry, your credit card, and your driver's license. Then, adding insult to injury, this person takes your keys and drives off in your car. Of course, the key ring contains all your keys, including the key to your home.

Now, imagine what your reaction would be as you are being robbed and then afterward. You may be panicked, frozen with fear, or disoriented. As you witness the taillights of your car disappear into the night, you may find your voice and cry out for help. Then, as days and weeks pass, your sense of outrage grows. You pressure the police to find the robber, all the while holding out hope that your possessions will be found and returned. You do not feel safe anymore, and you jump at the slightest noise.

Being robbed is not a neutral experience, and neither is bereavement. Like robbery, becoming bereaved leaves you in a different condition than before the death. Indeed, in the definition of bereavement found in the *Oxford English Dictionary*, being robbed describes the most central quality of becoming deprived. Similar words found in historical definitions of bereavement are *plundered* and *despoiled*. They convey the tragic quality that bereavement can sometimes assume, when death leaves a person destitute, orphaned, or widowed.

In bereavement, the robbery is always twofold. Life is stolen from the one who died, and the one who died is stolen from those who survive. Consequently, the emotional responses that come with bereavement reflect this dual robbery. For instance, you may be angry with the robber, death, for depriving you of your loved one, but you also may be filled with a strong sense of injustice that death has deprived your loved one of life. Or in a different circumstance, you may feel sad that you no longer have your friend, but simultaneously you may feel relieved that the awful suffering your friend experienced during a terminal illness is ended.

As you can see, this twofold robbery gives rise to numerous possible combinations of emotional responses depending on the people involved and the situation. The condition of being bereaved involves something more. Tangled up in emotional responses lies a heightened awareness of death itself, beyond the death of a specific person. Now, thoughts about your own death, the death of everyone, and the impermanence of all creation may force themselves upon you. You view death as a fact of life, and you see how it is viewed in contemporary culture and society. This confrontation with death leads to questions of meaning, justice, fairness, and the nature of life.

Finally, and not surprisingly, the issue of life and death leads to the question of God. Perennial questions with which human beings wrestle may arise as if they had never before been addressed. Why did God let this happen? Why didn't God answer our prayers? Was it God's will that our loved one died? How could God have created a world in which human beings have to suffer and die? In bereavement, people become Job, protesting their innocence and demanding an accounting of the unfair situation into which they have been thrown.

Finally, two additional features of bereavement must be introduced. They can best be explained with the help of another word commonly used for describing bereavement—*loss*.

Loss

Loss is a simple little word, but it conveys far more than you might think. In contemporary language, it can refer to many things besides situations involving death. For instance, loss can refer to misplacing something, like losing your umbrella. Or it can refer to being defeated in competition, such as losing a game of tennis. *Loss* also can refer to experiences approximating bereavement. For example, a person who loses a job because the company downsizes is deprived of something in which the person has made a significant emotional investment. In this sense, losing a job can be like entering the condition of bereavement. The same can be said for many other losses in life, such as losing custody of your child, losing friends and community, or losing a long-held dream. While the robber is not literal death, the condition of being deprived is real.

Not surprisingly, then, *loss* also can be used interchangeably with *bereavement* in situations involving literal death. Yet *loss* plays a more important role in the vocabulary of bereavement than just being a synonym of bereavement. Following the initial, primary loss due to death, the bereaved may experience additional losses occurring as a result of the initial loss. These are called secondary losses. They are part of bereavement considered as a whole (see Rando, 1993, 20). The ability of *loss* to refer to experiences approximating bereavement makes it ideal for referring to secondary losses within bereavement.

For instance, consider the situation when a spouse dies. The main loss, of course, is the loss of the person. Right away additional losses occur. The loss of a life partner brings the additional loss of ongoing companionship, as two people travel together on life's journey. In addition, the death may lead to the loss of income, depending on the situation, which in turn can lead to the loss of a home. The losses can just seem to pile up, each one bringing its own deprivation, as if insult keeps following injury.

The reality of secondary losses brings out yet another feature of bereavement, one addressed in some contemporary psychotherapy. This feature involves change to something new, which is the counterpart to becoming deprived of something lost. For instance, in the example of losing a spouse, if one secondary loss is losing companionship, the flip side of that loss involves learning how to live alone again out of necessity. This is not just an unwanted condition into which the bereaved person is thrown. Rather, it becomes a challenge, part of building a new life.

The Psychological Understanding of Grief and Mourning

When a tragedy happens, such as students being killed in a school shooting, the national press covers the story; and the nation watches on television and the Internet. One part of the story typically includes reporting that counselors are available to help survivors with their grief. Also, prominent psychotherapists may appear on talk shows to discuss grief and how to cope with it. Psychotherapists are the experts who teach society about bereavement today and for good reason. They have been developing the concepts of grief and mourning for many years, with the help of research and by practicing therapy with grieving clients. Learning what they have to say about grief and mourning is important for twenty-first–century congregations, as part of developing an understanding of bereavement that will inform the congregation's care of grieving people. In this section, then, I will discuss grief first, followed by mourning.

Grief

Grief refers to the reaction human beings have when they become bereaved. Dictionaries describe this reaction in various ways, such as intense sorrow, poignant distress, and deep mental anguish. While emotions associated with grief often are emphasized, today psychologists point out that grief is manifested in many areas of life, from physical reactions to social and behavioral changes.

In *Meaning Reconstruction & the Experience of Loss* (2001), psychotherapist Robert A. Neimeyer says that a major shift is occurring in the understanding of grief as the twentieth century gives way to the twenty-first. He characterizes this shift in terms of modern views of grief being replaced by postmodern ones. In a different book, Neimeyer and five coauthors give a helpful overview of contemporary grief theories (see Neimeyer, et al., 2002, 35–38). Let's look at some of the changing understandings of grief, because twenty-first–century pastors and congregations need to know about them.

The First Change. Neimeyer describes the modern understanding of bereavement, or grief, found in the twentieth century: "For most of the 20th century, bereavement was understood in quintessentially 'modern' terms, as a process of 'letting go' of one's attachment to the deceased person, 'moving on' with one's life, and gradually 'recovering' from the depression occasioned by the loss so as to permit a return to 'normal' behavior" (2001, 2).

In contrast, today the pendulum is swinging away from an emphasis on resolving grief by letting the deceased person go, moving on, recovering from depression, and returning to normal. It is swinging toward learning how to relate to the lost loved one in a new way as an ongoing part of life in the present, though this is not a new idea by any stretch of the imagination. Thomas Attig, in *The Heart of Grief: Death and the Search for Lasting Love*, describes the newfound emphasis this way: "The central challenge as we grieve is learning to love in a new way, to love someone in separation, at least as long as we walk this earth" (2000, 282).

The Second Change. Another swing of the pendulum is away from thinking of grief primarily in terms of stages through which every bereaved person is supposed to pass to return to normal. The most famous stage model associated with grief is found in the book, *On Death and Dying* (1969), by psychiatrist Elisabeth Kübler-Ross. As Neimeyer and others point out, scientific researchers are not finding universally experienced stages of grief, which is causing stage thinking about grief to be questioned and rejected. For example, Dennis Klass, writing about bereaved parents who have lost children, reflects this view when he says, "It seems reasonably well accepted today that there are no invariant stages in grief" (2001, 79).

As the twentieth century fades into history, the pendulum is swinging toward a heightened emphasis on respecting individuality in grieving. For instance, Harold I. Smith argues strongly that pastors who care for the bereaved should focus on individuality, or uniqueness, in grieving, because "every grief has right turns, left turns, U-turns, and dead ends. And when these occur, the pastor-leader is present to offer care" (2001, 44).

The Third Change. A third swing of the pendulum is away from what could be termed a passive view of grief characterized by such phrases as "going through" grief. Presumably, one is going through the stages. Instead, the pendulum is swinging toward a more proactive view of grief, like the feature of loss discussed earlier with the challenge to build a new life. Neimeyer places the proactive emphasis at the heart of grief, focusing on the active, constructive role of the mind in making meaning. He says that the central process of grieving is "meaning reconstruction in response to a loss" (2001, 4).

Reconstructing meaning has to do with the narrative, or story, of a grieving person's life. "Like a novel that loses a central character in the middle chapters, the life story disrupted by loss must be reorganized, rewritten, to find a new strand of continuity that bridges the past with the future in an intelligible fashion." This understanding of grief places a heavy emphasis on a contemporary postmodern understanding of language and its use. In this view, a grieving person necessarily draws on a preexisting fund of language, or discourse, for doing the rewriting, or for making new meaning in one's life. As Neimeyer says, "individuals make meaning by drawing selectively on a fund of discourse that precedes them and that is consensually validated within their cultures, subcultures, communities, and families" (2001, 263–264).

These swings of the pendulum reflect the way grief is coming to be understood in the twenty-first century. Grief involves learning a new way of relating to the deceased, as opposed to just learning to let go and move on. It involves individuality, as opposed to marching through universal stages. It involves proactively rewriting one's life story, as opposed to passively going through grief.

I will describe grieving as rewriting a bereaved life story, but I will elaborate such rewriting, or meaning reconstruction, in terms of mourning processes seen in relation to spirituality associated with the lament psalms, discussed in each of the following chapters. Mourning will provide a psychological language for discussing the bereaved person's proactive efforts to address the grief during the beginning, the middle, and the eventual concluding part of the rewriting. In other words, mourning will show what the rewriting needs to be about during different periods of grieving and the reasons for this. For example, chapter 3 is about the beginning of grief. In that chapter, the first mourning process associated with the beginning of grief shows what the rewriting needs to be about as grief begins. Likewise, the psalms of lament will provide a spiritual language for discussing the rewriting throughout the time of grieving. The psalms will show the proactive character of grieving by revealing the intentional, purposeful, and multifaceted ways that bereaved people may relate to God as they experience the different mourning processes.

Mourning

Like the other words being discussed, *mourning* has relatively simple dictionary definitions, such as feeling and expressing deep sadness over a loss, longing for one who has been lost, and engaging in ceremonial expressions of loss. Mourning also has a long tradition in psychology, beginning with Sigmund Freud's use of the word in his famous essay, "Mourning and Melancholia."

During the last half-century, psychotherapists and others who write about bereavement have discussed the relationship between mourning and grief in a variety of ways. Often, grief and mourning are seen as different words for the same thing. However, they also are viewed as representing different parts of the same thing. In this case, grief is viewed as the subjective, internal reaction to loss, while mourning is seen as the external expression of that reaction. One kind of external expression of grief is immediate and spontaneous, such as crying due to sorrow. The sorrow is the internal grief reaction, and crying is the external expression of the grief reaction. Finally, another kind of external expression of grief is a ritual, or ceremonial, expression, which is why people at a funeral are called mourners.

Increasingly, mourning is being discussed in a different way. Recall the discussion of psychiatrist Eric Lindemann in chapter 1. In his concept of grief work, grieving patients work on their grief with the assistance of the psychiatrist. Mourning is a more contemporary way of describing what the grieving person must do to negotiate grief in a healthy manner. Some models describe this as a series of tasks. Other models describe it as a series of processes. While mourning processes happen at an unconscious level, they also include conscious behaviors. In this sense, contemporary mourning and grief share an emphasis on the grieving person being proactive.

For example, Neimeyer indicates that rewriting a bereaved life story, or meaning reconstruction, has a constructive purpose, enabling the grieving person to find a new strand of continuity bridging the past with the future. Likewise, as I discussed above, mourning can provide a psychological way of describing those processes that need to happen for the rewriting to be accomplished. In a sense, mourning fleshes out the metaphor of rewriting through its series of processes. In this regard, it is perhaps appropriate that long ago *process* could be a word for narrating something, such as a story. It also could mean narrative, and a passage in a narrative such as a biblical passage, according to the *Oxford English Dictionary*.

Dictionaries also tell us that a process involves a series of actions heading toward some result. The model of mourning psychologist Therese Rando developed in her book *Treatment of Complicated Mourning* (1993) involves six mourning processes. She calls these the R processes, because they all begin with the letter R. This model can be helpful to pastors and congregations in the ministry of lament, and it will provide the main content for the psychological part of the conversation with the psalms of lament. Here is a brief overview of the six mourning processes:

Recognize the Loss. Rando says the first part of grief is characterized by a desire to avoid acknowledging the loss. The initial mourning process counters this understandable desire. One of its main aspects involves acknowledging that the death has happened, but this is just the barest, most minimal acknowledgement (1993, 44).

React to the Separation. This mourning process follows logically from the first one. When the death is acknowledged, reacting to it and coping with it begins in myriad ways, such as experiencing and handling increasing pain (Rando, 1993, 47).

Recollect and Reexperience the Deceased and the Relationship. The third mourning process involves reminiscing about the deceased at an emotional level. This is important for beginning to change the relationship with the deceased to one that will be ongoing in the present (Rando, 1993, 48–49).

Relinquish the Old Attachments to the Deceased and the Old Assumptive World. The fourth mourning process involves examining old attachments, or ties, to the deceased, along with old assumptions associated with the deceased. These are ties and assumptions that must be relinquished so they can be replaced with new ones reflecting the reality of the death (Rando, 1993, 50).

Readjust to Move Adaptively into the New World without Forgetting the Old. The fifth mourning process involves becoming increasingly accustomed to living in the present in many different areas of life, while finding ways to accommodate the loss, making room for the loss as part of living a healthy life in the present. Rando emphasizes that all the change going on does not mean that connections to the past must be gone (1993, 52).

Reinvest. The final mourning process involves a certain type of investment, but not one of money. Rather, emotional energy formerly invested in the relationship with the deceased must be reinvested in rewarding new relationships, pursuits, activities, and so forth. Rando makes clear that no new investments can replace the deceased and that part of the reinvested energy goes toward the mourner's present relationship with the deceased (1993, 60).

Mourning is the psychological conversation partner that I will bring into dialogue with the psalms of lament. Now, let's turn to the psalms.

Introducing the Psalms of Lament

Biblical study is the most natural thing in the world for a pastor and congregation. This introduction to the psalms of lament will present several insights from biblical scholars; each one is something congregations need to know about the psalms of lament in the service of caring for the bereaved and as preparation for the dialogue between these psalms and mourning.

You may never have thought about what the word *psalm* actually means. According to Nancy deClaissé-Walford, the word *psalm* simply means *hymn*. Any churchgoer knows that in worship you sing hymns, which are religious songs of praise to God. Of course, unlike ancient Israel, contemporary Christians do not typically sing the psalms in worship. Instead, they are read as scripture (2004, 2).

Psalms Are Scripture

The book of Psalms is sometimes called the Psalter, which may be new to you if you never have read much about the psalms. A psalter, says deClaissé-Walford, is "a printed collection of hymns." Whether we refer to the book of Psalms or to the Psalter, we are referring to the same thing, a printed collection of songs in which worshipers sing praise to God (2004, 2). James L. Crenshaw, notes that the word *psalter* derives from an ancient musical instrument.

Presumably, this instrument was used to accompany psalm singing (2001, 3).

The collection of psalms into a book is not random. Scholars have shown its shape to be purposeful. For instance, the Psalter is divided into five sections, or books, the first book containing Psalms 1 through 41. Scholars suggest that this fivefold division reflects the Pentateuch, the first five books of the Bible, but this is not just an imitation.

The Pentateuch contains the law, or the Torah in Hebrew. Clinton McCann finds that if the shape of the Psalter as scripture is taken seriously, the concept of the Torah is elevated to "central significance in understanding the Psalms." He demonstrates this through his analysis of Psalm 1, the psalm that introduces the whole Psalter (1993, 25).

In the first verse, the psalmist poetically cites several possible guides for living that are best left alone:

> Happy are those
>   who do not follow the advice of the wicked,
> or take the path that sinners tread,
>   or sit in the seat of scoffers;

Then, in verse 2, we find the recommended guide:

> but their delight is in the law of the Lord,
>   and on his law they meditate day and night.

If this law, or Torah, the "law of the LORD," were understood simply as divine commands to be obeyed, or rigid rules to be followed, the person doing the obeying would be going down the road of an insufferable legalism, in which case the Psalter "does not sound too promising or inviting" (McCann, 1992, 118). Instead, McCann argues that the Torah must be understood differently as it pertains to the psalms. "The introduction to the Psalter is anything but an invitation to pedantry, legalism, or self-righteousness. On the contrary, it is an invitation to be *open to God's instruction*" (1993, 27).

This divine instruction, the "law of the LORD," is not just found in Psalm 1 or other psalms that mention the law. Instead, as an introduction to the whole Psalter, Psalm 1 "invites the reader to receive all the material which follows in the book of Psalms as a source of God's instruction" (McCann, 1992, 119).

The lament psalms contain the material best enabling pastors and congregations to seek "God's instruction" regarding the care of bereaved people. God is the teacher, and the congregation is the student. This is the first thing that needs to be known about the psalms of lament. The second thing is understanding what kind of literature the psalms are.

Psalms Are Poetry

During the early part of the twentieth century, Hermann Gunkel did groundbreaking research on the psalms. In 1967, some his work appeared in an English edition entitled, *The Psalms: A Form-Critical Introduction*. He sees that the Psalms comprises "an important kind of religious poetry" and entitles a chapter, "Liturgical Poetry," as he begins exploring how the ancient Israelites used the psalms in worship (1967, 4).

Since Gunkel's time, the psalms have received much study as poetry. Indeed, one contemporary school of biblical scholarship called rhetorical criticism focuses on the literature of the psalms, analyzing their poetic features. Ironically, however, the poetic nature of the psalms can seem lost when a psalm, or a small part of a psalm, is read as scripture in worship today. Contemporary congregations need to rediscover the Psalms' poetic nature. If nothing else, the constant bombardment of imagery throughout the Psalter should be a strong clue to their poetry. For instance, one of the most famous psalms, Psalm 23, begins:

> The LORD is my shepherd, I shall not want.
>   He makes me lie down in green pastures;
> he leads me beside still waters;
>   he restores my soul.

Obviously we are in poetic territory here. The Lord is not literally a human shepherd, nor are you literally a sheep who lies down in pastures and drinks out of a gentle stream.

Churches have de-emphasized the psalms in worship during recent times, especially the psalms of lament (see Brueggemann, 1995, 102–11). Apparently, scholars tend to assume that pastors and church members want to avoid hearing troubling expressions of pain and suffering. Nancy Duff, for instance, criticizes society and the church for discouraging people "from expressing intense feelings of sorrow or anger when we experience a significant loss in our lives" (2005, 5). Duff, however, fails to consider the societal support for psychotherapy as the setting in which Americans are encouraged to express their suffering. Nor does she consider the participation of the church in this support through pastoral care and counseling, as discussed in chapter 1.

Other reasons lead churches to avoid the psalms of lament in worship. I have to wonder if the book of Psalms' poetic nature plays a significant role in their avoidance. Singing poetic lyrics is one thing. Listening to a poem being read is another. In American society, during a time when even many popular songs have mundane prose for lyrics, listening to poetry may become a trial, if not a tribulation, for those whose ears are not attuned to the imagery and cadences of poetry. Nor does reading a brief portion of a psalm in church make it any easier to hear, because the worship leader may read the psalm as if it were a dry narrative rather than attending to the rhythm inherent in the poetry of the psalm.

If the psalms of lament are going to help a congregation in its care of the bereaved, their character as poetry must be acknowledged and accepted. Exploring poetry that expresses deep pain and suffering, as well as praise, opens up a new and powerful world of meaning that is extremely relevant for those who grieve and for those who care for the bereaved. William Brown writes:

> The power of Psalms lies first and foremost in its evocative use of language. The psalms at once caress and assault the soul. They orient, disorient, and reorient; they scale the heights of praise as well as plumb the depths of despair...As poetry, the psalms

do not simply express; they also impart and teach…
Biblical poetry is poetry with a purpose. (2002, 2)

So far, the focus has been on the book of Psalms as a whole. Now, the focus narrows to the psalms of lament specifically.

Lament: What Does It Mean?

Biblical scholars hardly ever define and explain lament. It will be helpful to take a look at this word. According to the *Oxford English Dictionary*, a lament is a certain kind of act, "a passionate or demonstrative expression of grief." Note that this is not a meek or mild expression of grief. It is a bold, deeply and intensely felt expression, the kind that may extend all the way to weeping and wailing. Psalm 31:9–10, provides an excellent example of a lament:

> Be gracious to me, O LORD, for I am in distress;
>   my eye wastes away from grief,
>   my soul and body also.
> For my life is spent with sorrow,
>   and my years with sighing;
> my strength fails because of my misery,
>   and my bones waste away.

The dictionary also tells us that a lament may be understood as a "set or conventional form of mourning." One such form is singing, in which a lament is a song of grief called an elegy. One kind of elegy is a dirge. A dirge is a song sung in commemoration of the dead, or simply a song of mourning performed at a death or burial. An elegy also can take the form of poetry.

As much as a lament addresses situations involving death, it cannot be confined to bereavement, just as grief and mourning do not just address literal death. People lament, grieve, and mourn many different things. One can lament a favorite team losing in the playoffs, for instance. Likewise, one cannot confine the psalms of lament to situations involving the literal death of a person. They address a variety of issues, such as physical illness and emotional trauma. Even so, they speak profoundly to bereavement, but not solely about expressing suffering, as the form of the psalms of lament will allow us to see.

Psalms of Lament: Their Form

The Psalter features several different types of psalms, as Hermann Gunkel pointed out in *The Psalms: A Form-Critical Introduction*. Some are hymns praising God. Others give thanks. Royal psalms speak about kings. Some focus specifically on the king being enthroned. Some psalms deal with creation; others deal with wisdom. Among all the different types of psalms, however, those named psalms of lament are the largest group. Some of them are laments of the community, and some are laments of individuals.

The lament psalms have a distinctive form, or structure. In his book *Out of the Depths: The Psalms Speak for Us Today* (2000), Bernhard W. Anderson says the psalms of lament have a six-part structure. I will present a brief outline of this structure, because it will provide the main biblical content in the conversation with mourning. Keep in mind, however, that not every psalm of lament contains each part. Nor do the different parts stand out in many psalms. Sometimes a particular part of the psalm is hard to discern, and other times it appears at a different point in the psalm than usual.

Address to God. The lament psalms begin with the person or community speaking to God. This is a clue that the Psalms are written prayers. The particular way that the psalmist addresses God lets the reader know immediately that the psalm will not be a happy one. According to Anderson, this address is "a brief cry," but it may be expanded to include some praise or even some recounting of God's past deeds (2000, 61).

For instance, Psalm 22 begins with a cry to God in verses 1–2:

My God, my God, why have you forsaken me?
　Why are you so far from helping me, from the
　　words of my groaning?

O my God, I cry by day, but you do not answer;
and by night but find no rest.

This is, perhaps, the most well-known address to God in the lament psalms, because Jesus quotes the first line of this psalm while he is being crucified (Mark 15:34).

Complaint. Once God is addressed, the psalmist wastes no time getting right to a grievance, dissatisfaction, pain, or troubling situation. According to Anderson, community complaints can be anything from a military crisis to a famine. Individual complaints include sickness, threats from enemies, and other disturbing circumstances. Some complaints are associated with guilt, and these have become known as penitential psalms. In others, however, the complaint includes a protest of innocence (2000, 61).

Continuing with Psalm 22, the psalmist in verses 6–8 complains about being scorned, despised, and mocked:

But I am a worm, and not human;
scorned by others, and despised by the people.
All who see me mock at me;
they make mouths at me, they shake their heads;
'Commit your cause to the Lord; let him deliver—
let him rescue the one in whom he delights!'

Confession of Trust. This part of the lament psalm may seem surprising. Right after the complaint, the psalmist expresses confidence in God. This sudden transition may be introduced by a "but" or "nevertheless" right after the complaint (Anderson, 2000, 61).

The confession of trust in Psalm 22 appears in verses 9–10:

Yet it was you who took me from the womb;
you kept me safe on my mother's breast.
On you I was cast from my birth,
and since my mother bore me you have been my
God.

Petition. Following the confession of trust in God, the psalmist petitions God, making an appeal or request for intervention and deliverance. Anderson says that in some psalms of lament, the psalmist includes reasons supporting the petition (2000, 61).

Psalm 22 contains a brief petition in verse 11:

> Do not be far from me,
> > for trouble is near
> > and there is no one to help.

Immediately, in verses 12–18, this petition is followed by a dramatic elaboration of the psalmist's condition supporting the petition. Evildoers are portrayed as bulls and dogs menacingly surrounding the troubled person, whose heart is like wax, melted within the breast. Things are so bad that the evildoers even cast lots for the clothes of the psalmist who has become emaciated, another scene found in Jesus' crucifixion. Then, in verses 19–21, the psalmist expands the petition.

Words of Assurance. In this part of the psalm, says Anderson, the earlier confession of trust now finds expression "in the certainty that the prayer will be heard" (2000, 61). In Psalm 22, in the second half of verse 21, the psalmist expresses assurance of being rescued:

> From the horns of the wild oxen you have rescued me.

The psalmist expands this in verse 24 with assurance that God has heard the prayer:

> For he did not despise or abhor
> > the affliction of the afflicted;
> he did not hide his face from me,
> > but heard when I cried to him.

Vow of Praise and Thanksgiving. Following assurance comes the end of the psalm characterized by exclamations of praise. According to Anderson, the petitioner "vows to call upon the name of God and to testify before the community what Yhwh has done" (2000, 62). In Psalm 22, the vow of praise and thanksgiving is exceptional. In verse 25, the psalmist vows to praise and give thanks through a thank offering in the congregation:

From you comes my praise in the great congregation;
my vows I will pay before those who fear him.

The vow of praise and thanksgiving expands to include
people everywhere in verses 27–28. Finally, the vow expands
extraordinarily to all generations in verses 29–31.

The Dialogue

In conclusion, I present below a brief outline showing
how the conversation between the two partners will take
place. The six mourning processes of Rando will represent
the psychological conversation partner. The six-part form
of the lament psalms, as put forth by Bernhard Anderson,
will represent the biblical conversation partner. Other
psychological and biblical scholarship will be brought into
the conversation as needed, but these will be the main two.

Psychological Mourning and Biblical Lament

PSYCHOLOGICAL MOURNING	BIBLICAL LAMENT
Recognize the Loss	Address to God
React to the Separation	Complaint
Recollect and Reexperience the Deceased and the Relationship	Confession of Trust
Relinquish the Old Attachments to the Deceased and the Old Assumptive World	Petition
Readjust to Move Adaptively into the New World without Forgetting the Old	Words of Assurance
Reinvest	Vow of Praise and Thanksgiving

The next chapter presents the first mourning process,
recognize the loss, along with the first part of the lament
psalms, address to God. Then, in each chapter that follows,
the next part of the conversation will take place.

CHAPTER 3

Discovering Death and Crying Out to God

All who mourn have the beginning of grief in common. Grief occurs when a person first learns about the death of a family member, friend, or someone with whom the person shares an emotional tie. This beginning grief lasts for only a relatively brief time. The initial mourning process relates to the beginning of grief, so this part of grief will be discussed briefly. Next, I will present the first mourning process, followed by the initial part of the lament psalms. The third part of the chapter relates mourning and the lament psalms to newly bereaved people in the congregational setting. Finally, I will draw implications for the ministry of lament

Grief at Its Beginning

Rando calls the first part of grief the avoidance phase, marked by "the understandable desire to avoid the terrible acknowledgment that the loved one is lost." In concert with many who have written about grief, she describes what is happening at this time psychologically as the experience of shock followed by denial. In shock, the person receives a blow that may result in such things as emotional numbness and bewilderment. "In brief, the mourner is reeling from the news." Then, as shock begins to wear off, denial replaces it. The reality of the death is temporarily denied to some extent.

Denial, says Rando, acts as a "buffer, allowing the mourner to absorb the reality of the loss gradually over time and serving as emotional anesthesia while the mourner begins to experience the painful awareness of the loss" (1993, 33).

Individual reactions occur during this time. It would seem strange, for instance, if all family members experienced the death of a loved one in exactly the same manner. One family member may seem disoriented and confused, while another rises to the occasion and takes charge of funeral arrangements. Different individuals may experience a wide variety of intense emotions, and some may have periodic emotional outbursts. Others may experience a lack of emotion, becoming withdrawn, or experiencing their actions as mechanical (Rando, 1993, 33).

Joan Didion tells about the night her husband died of a heart attack as she prepared dinner. The paramedics arrived and took her husband to the local hospital emergency room. After she had waited in the reception area, a social worker ushered her into a room. After further wait, the social worker reappeared, now with a medical doctor: "There was a silence. 'He's dead, isn't he,' I heard myself say to the doctor. The doctor looked at the social worker. 'It's okay,' the social worker said. 'She's a pretty cool customer'" (2007, 15). This may have been a poor choice of words by the social worker, but he does represent Didion as emotionally calm. As the rest of the book shows, however, you would make a grave mistake to assume she was any less devastated than another person who may have cried hysterically in a similar circumstance.

The First Mourning Process: Recognize the Loss

Rando names the first mourning process recognizing the loss. This process involves acknowledging and understanding the loss in certain rudimentary ways. A newly bereaved person, having just begun grieving, may desperately want to avoid acknowledging the reality of the death. Mourning requires that this strong desire ultimately give way to recognizing the loss in the sense of coming to grips with the bare fact that it actually has occurred.

Acknowledge the Death. Wanting to avoid acknowledging a death at the beginning of grief does not mean that the newly bereaved person has no awareness of it. Rather, it can mean that the person is not yet able to concede the fact of the death. When the new mourner does acknowledge the death, this person is yielding to the truth, conceding that it has happened, even if this acknowledgment is the most minimalist concession. As Rando puts it, "this acceptance is on an intellectual level, involving only recognition and concession of the fact of the death." Acknowledgement at deeper levels then can happen as time passes (1993, 44).

Wanting to avoid acknowledging the death is perfectly normal at the beginning of grief, but letting avoidance become a way of life leads to trouble down the road, because conceding the fact of the death is necessary for grief to occur. The natural urge to deny the death and avoid dealing with it is so strong that having evidence of the death is very important. According to Rando, this is "why so much time, money, and effort are spent attempting to recover bodies after airplane crashes, boating accidents, earthquakes, and so forth." Without evidence of the death, those who lose loved ones can "postpone their mourning or rationalize it away" (1993, 44).

A similar situation can occur when a person does not know whether a loved one is dead or alive. Rando gives the example of a woman who reasonably thought that her husband probably died on a canoeing expedition when his raft overturned. Yet for months she lived in a kind of holding pattern, making no changes in her life. "Although she 'sort of knew' in her head, she could not allow herself to mourn. She felt it would be tantamount to giving up on her husband." Finally, however, evidence of her husband's death turned up on the riverbank, when a set of dentures was found and were proved to be his. At long last, his wife became free to plan a memorial service and begin to grieve actively (1993, 46).

In addition to acknowledging the death, a mourner also needs to know that the death was due to a particular cause, whether by illness or accident. Rando calls this understanding the death.

Understand the Death. Understanding a death can occur at different levels, such as a profound philosophical understanding. It also can be understood from different perspectives, such as medically and religiously. What Rando has in mind in the first mourning process is much more simple, immediate, and practical, having to do with reasons for the death. The reasons, she writes, "concern the facts contributing to the death and the circumstances surrounding it. The explanation needs to make sense intellectually, but it does not necessarily have to be acceptable to the survivor" (1993, 46).

The mourner has a good reason for needing to understand how a loved one died. Even in the best of circumstances, human beings "have a powerful need for comprehension—for cognitive mastery, predictability, and control—and the security provided by what is logical and sensible. The world needs to be perceived as having some order if the individual is to go on in a healthy way" (Rando, 1993, 398).

Not knowing how a loved one died contributes to undermining the need for control and order. Consequently, says Rando, without understanding the cause of death, "a mourner tends to become anxious and confused, wondering about what happened to her loved one and what potentially could happen to her" (1993, 46–47).

Pastors and congregations need to know the first mourning process. They also need to know the first part of the lament psalms to practice the ministry of lament.

The First Part of the Lament Psalms: The Address to God

Anne Lamott tells about an incident when she was teaching in a writing conference in Idaho. She had to decide whether or not to allow her almost seven-year-old son Sam to accept an offer to go paragliding in a harness with an adult, one of the most qualified people in the area. This man had been taking his son paragliding with him since his son was five years old. She was torn and could not decide. Finally, she consulted with friends, which did not help. "Half said I should let Sam go; half acted as if I were considering buying Sam a chain saw for his birthday. All the ones who believe in God told me to pray, so I did." Lamott then makes a comment about prayer that, on the one hand, is funny, but, on the other hand, is profound. She writes: "Here are the two best prayers I know: 'Help me, help me, help me,' and 'Thank you, thank you, thank you'" (1999, 82).

This may be the most succinct explanation of the lament psalms ever written, because the psalms of lament contain both "Help me" and "Thank you." The first part of the lament psalms initiates the "Help me, help me, help me" part of the psalm.

Anderson names the initial part of the lament psalms the address to God. As we saw in chapter 2, the address is a brief cry to God. It is urgent, not a calm utterance. Right away the psalmist is letting God know that something serious is happening and that God is needed now! In addition to the cry, the psalmist may shift gears and add some praise, or recount God's past deeds (2000, 61).

Take some time to linger over the following addresses to God in the lament psalms. Remember, they are poetry:

Psalm 5:1–3
Give ear to my words, O Lord;
    give heed to my sighing.
Listen to the sound of my cry,
    my King and my God,
    for to you I pray.
O Lord, in the morning you hear my voice;
    in the morning I plead my case to you, and watch.

Psalm 13:1
How long, O Lord? Will you forget me forever?
    How long will you hide your face from me?

Psalm 28:1–2
To you, O Lord, I call;
    my rock do not refuse to hear me,
for if you are silent to me,

I shall be like those who go down to the Pit.
Hear the voice of my supplication,
> as I cry to you for help,
as I lift up my hands
> toward your most holy sanctuary.

Psalm 55:1–2a
Give ear to my prayer, O God;
> do not hide yourself from my supplication.
Attend to me, and answer me.

Psalm 80:1–3
Give ear, O Shepherd of Israel,
> you who lead Joseph like a flock!
You who are enthroned upon the cherubim, shine forth
> before Ephraim and Benjamin and Manasseh.
Stir up your might,
> and come to save us!

These illustrations show that psalms of lament begin as the psalmist addresses God. They also show that the word *address* is a bit tame to capture the quality of speaking to God in the lament psalms. Every call to God in the psalms of lament contains a real sense of urgency. It is like saying, "God, listen to me! Something extremely serious is going on, and I need your help!" Or simply, "Help me, help me, help me."

The lament psalms convey their urgency with poetic power and beauty, as Psalm 5:1–3 above conveys. Instead of just writing prosaically, "Please listen to me, Lord," the psalmist writes:

Give ear to my words, O Lord;
> give heed to my sighing.

This "sighing" is not a sigh of relief, but conveys a plea to be heard at deeper levels than mere words. The psalmist continues:

Listen to the sound of my cry,
> my King and my God,
> for to you I pray.

A cry surpasses the sigh. Some kind of pain or suffering requires immediate attention, so the psalmist persists. This suffering person will keep crying out to God every morning until God does hear and respond:

> O Lord, in the morning you hear my voice;
>   in the morning I plead my case to you, and watch.

Imagery of God's Anatomy and Response to the Psalmist

From the beginning of the prayer, the psalmist is conversing with God quite actively. The psalmist wants God to hear, remember, save, invoke justice, protect, and speak. God is treated like a person who is listening. William Brown points out that psalmic imagery portrays God as a person actively engaged with the psalmist, one who is quite capable of hearing, seeing, and responding to the cry of the psalmist. For instance, God is portrayed as having bodily senses, such as sight and hearing associated with eyes and ears. These highlight God's "perceptiveness and responsiveness to situations of distress" (2002, 169–170).

In Psalm 94, for example, the psalmist has strong complaints against enemies who deny that God sees or perceives their unethical and harmful behavior. In verses 8–11, the psalmist responds to the enemies:

> Understand, O dullest of the people;
>   fools, when will you be wise?
> He who planted the ear, does he not hear?
> He who formed the eye, does he not see?
> He who disciplines the nations,
> he who teaches knowledge to humankind,
>   does he not chastise?
> The Lord knows our thoughts,
>   that they are but an empty breath.

Brown goes on to discuss imagery involving God's face, signifying God's presence and the yearning of the psalmist to interact with God. He discusses God's powerful hand, God's mouth and voice, God's life-giving breath, and God's emotions, including everything from anger and hatred, to love, compassion, and delight/pleasure. Finally, Brown discusses the imagery and situations associated with God's memory and its importance for the psalmist (2002, 172–187).

If the poetic imagery of the lament psalms portrays the psalmist and the troubling situation in graphic terms, it portrays God just as graphically. God is quite capable of entering into conversation no matter how intense or desperate the cry. Do not forget: The psalms of lament are poetry as well as prayer!

Mourners as Contemporary Psalmists of Lament

In this section, and in the rest of the book, grieving people who are rewriting their bereaved life story are presented as contemporary psalmists of lament. Because the rewriting includes spirituality, mourners become poets who pray to God. In one sense, rewriting in the realm of the spiritual life can be seen as rewriting in just one area of the mourner's life among others. This view contains some truth because mourners may be wrestling with their relationship to God, and the focus in prayer may need to be on that relationship specifically. This view also can falsely separate spirituality from the rest of life. Instead, mourners bring any and all aspects of their life to God in prayer, and their wrestling with God is not separated from this.

Relating the first mourning process to the first part of the lament psalms shows how newly bereaved people begin their psalm of lament. Recognizing the loss, the first mourning process, provides the content informing the address to God. For instance, a newly bereaved person may pray:

God, don't let it be true!

This reflects the strong desire to avoid acknowledging the death. Conceding the fact of the death takes a great deal of courage. Through the fog of shock and denial, the death makes itself known. Deep down, it may be impossible to believe that the dead person will not return at this point; but the denial is only partial. In this case, the address to God may be a cry for God to hear and help the person have courage in the face of what is a monumental struggle to concede the fact of the death:

Lord, I don't know how I'm going to handle this;
will you give me the courage to face it?

The second part of the mourning process, understanding the death, also may give rise to the address to God. In many instances, the reasons for the death seem quite clear. Yet questions always can arise: What if the doctors failed to do something that could have prevented the lungs from filling with fluid? Was it really an accident, or was foul play involved? What will an autopsy reveal? Was it a suicide, or did the gun go off by accident? Was it an overdose, or was an illness being kept secret?

The address to God may include a cry for God to hear the person and help in understanding the death:

God, please listen!
They can't tell us for sure what happened,
but I can't let it go.
I need to know how she died!

We must take into account the diversity of emotional reaction. One person may be like Joan Didion, the "cool customer." Another, however, may cry right at the beginning of the death. The first mourning process, the need to acknowledge and understand the death in the face of powerful psychological forces designed to protect the person from the full impact of what happened, plays out in conjunction with this emotional diversity. The address to God must be taken seriously whether it is emotional or whether it is calm.

Addressing God

The biblical psalmists of lament show that it is perfectly acceptable to express urgency, distress, and persistence right at the beginning of prayer. So often, however, prayers begin in a perfunctory way, with a "Dear Lord" or an "O God," as if the one praying were writing God a mundane letter. This may be just fine when times are good and life is calm. The lament psalms, however, show that prayer can begin in quite a different manner when times are bad and life is anything but calm. As the biblical psalmists of lament address God, they seek God's attention in an urgent situation. Like the psalmist, a newly bereaved person needs the freedom to be honest and urgent in prayer right from the beginning.

Consider, as an example, *Psalms of Lament*, by Ann Weems. In the preface to her book, she tells part of her story as a newly bereaved person:

> On August 14, 1982, the stars fell from my sky. My son, my Todd, had been killed less than an hour after his twenty-first birthday. August 14, 1982... and still I weep...Many were there for me...family, friends, and people I didn't even know who sent their loving-kindness by mail or phone or in person. These tenderhearted ones were God-sent, and they have no idea how deeply they walked into my heart. (1995, xv)

The content of Weems' book contains psalms of lament that she wrote, as she mourned the death of her son. These psalms begin with the address to God. Here are some examples:

> O God, have you forgotten my name?
> How long will you leave me in this pit? (1995, 1)

> O Holy One, I can no longer see.
> Blinded by tears
> that will not cease,
> I can only cry out to you
> and listen
> for your footsteps. (1995, 7)

> Come to me, O God;
> set me free from this agony.
> O God, O God, O God,
> please help me! (1995, 15)

These ways of addressing God all make sense in the context of the grief and mourning that gripped Weems. When, for example, she prays to be set free from "from this agony," this agony certainly has to do with her grief and mourning.

Affirming new mourners as contemporary psalmists of lament conveys to them that praying for oneself is acceptable. More than a few people have no trouble praying for others and ministering to others in times of trial, but they feel that praying for oneself during a difficult time is selfish. The psalms of lament illustrate that seeking God's help during the beginning of grief and mourning is indeed acceptable.

Implications for the Ministry of Lament

Normally, at this point I would address pre-funeral pastoral visits, the funeral, and care for a brief time after the funeral. However, I have discussed this extensively in *Caring Through the Funeral: A Pastor's Guide,* which includes an emphasis on the beginning of grief and relating the first mourning process to the Christian funeral. I will not repeat that discussion here. One point about funerals needs to be made, however.

Funerals are the most important means of caring for the bereaved during the initial part of grief and mourning. Sadly, books on grief often stereotype mourners who attend funerals. They commonly portray mourners as so traumatized that they have little or no memory of the funeral or memorial service. Only weeks or months later do they begin emerging from the haze so that they can begin to mourn properly. Grief authors may then tend to lament that the mourner could not take advantage of the benefits afforded by the funeral.

Without doubt, some mourners are severely traumatized due to the nature of the death, and the funeral can be a blur. Pastors know this, and I do not want to downplay this reality at all. However, as pastors also know, shock and denial associated with the beginning of grief has many gradations. Mourners often do remember funerals, even in situations when loss is profound. Funerals often become memories for life, sacred memories, and some part of the service may be remembered as having special meaning—a song, a scripture passage, the memories or poem of a relative who speaks, a story in the sermon. Therefore, understanding grief at its beginning, along with the first part of mourning associated with it, is important for the ministry of caring for the bereaved.

In addition to funerals, prayer is a significant part of caring for newly bereaved people. The lament psalms provide an understanding of prayer that can guide pastors and the congregation in their prayers for the bereaved. While a point made about prayer may seem familiar or obvious to some, others may need to grow in their understanding of prayer so that their care of the bereaved will be enhanced. In any case, reflecting on the meaning of prayer and how it may be exercised in caring for the bereaved at the beginning of grief can be helpful.

How Prayer Starts

James L. Mays points out that the address to God at the beginning of the lament psalms teaches that prayer begins with the name of God. "In fact, the designation for prayer in the Psalms is 'to call on the name of the Lord'…Prayer cannot begin without this identification, this evocation, this recognition of the one spoken to" (2006, 8).

Just as a contemporary psalmist of lament begins prayer with a cry to God, so pastors and church members can address God with the same kind of honesty. This is appropriate, because the need to acknowledge the death and understand it informs the content of prayers for the mourner. Moreover, the pastor or church member who is praying also may be mourning the loss. The one who died may have been a friend for years, and the pastor or church member also needs to acknowledge the death and understand it.

Praying for a newly bereaved person or family does not have to keep to the well-worn openings of prayer that get said over and over, such as "Dear Lord." Instead, the cry to God can be a real cry, as simple as "Lord, hear us!" Getting away from whatever well-worn beginnings of prayer a pastor or church members may tend to say can help prayer be meaningful to a newly bereaved person, family, and friends of the one, or ones, who died. Such a cry says that the new suffering is being taken seriously and is accepted rather than rejected. It also may be that mourning is finding expression for the first time.

Conversation Based on Faith

Calling on the name of the Lord reveals how the psalmist and God are communicating in the prayer. The psalmist addresses God as a conversation partner identified and recognized as the one to whom the psalmist is speaking. Mays says that talking to God like you are talking to another person is "an astonishing act. It has rightly been called the supreme enactment of faith" (2006, 9).

Here we again pick up the story of Anne Lamott trying to decide whether or not to allow her son to go paragliding, because it contains a helpful point about faith. Her initial prayer does not resolve her dilemma. Then she begins remembering some things related to faith. When she wakes up the next morning, she remembers a poem about faith. Later, during dinner, after she tells friends about her dilemma, she remembers pastor Veronica's sermon that used a certain image to convey what faith is like:

> A memory came to me then, of our pastor Veronica telling us just the week before how she gets direction from God in prayer; she said that when she prays for direction, one spot of illumination always appears just beyond her feet, a circle of light into which she can step. She moved away from the pulpit to demonstrate, stepping forward shyly—this big-boned African-American woman tramping like Charlie Chaplin into an imagined spotlight, and then, after standing there looking puzzled, she moved another step forward to where the light had gone, two feet ahead of where she had been standing, and then again. 'We in our faith work,' she said, 'stumble along toward where

we think we're supposed to go, bumbling along, and here is what's so amazing—we end up getting exactly where we're supposed to be.' (1999, 84)

In the ministry of lament, prayer is understood as conversation with God. It is an act of faith, like stepping into the circle of light that moves you forward just a bit. From there, the circle of light may move again. Without stepping into the first circle of illumination, you will not have a next step to take.

Servant and Lord

Beginning prayer by calling on God not only reveals how the psalmist and God are communicating, but it also reveals who the conversation partners are in relation to one another. The psalmist is conversing with God as Lord, the one who is "sovereign, the one in whose power one's life is lived." Conversely, addressing God establishes the psalmist as a servant of the Lord. "In the vocabulary of Scripture, whoever calls another 'lord' is that one's servant. In the biblical literature 'servant' simply means one whose identity and doing is defined by a relation to another…So in calling on the name of the Lord, we are also saying something about ourselves" (Mays, 2006, 9–10).

Likewise, pastors and church members who practice the ministry of lament by praying for those who mourn are placing themselves in the position of being servants of God as Lord. Moreover, when pastors and church members hear and affirm prayers of mourners, or mourners tell about prayers they have prayed, they are seen as servants of the Lord implicitly.

Importance of the Name

Addressing God is not just the prelude to the important part of the conversation coming later. "In a profound sense, the entire essence of prayer is contained in the name spoken. In time of great stress and consternation of soul the believer may lack the words to compose a prayer and can only say the one word of the name (Lord, God), yet in the simple utterance of the name, prayer is made. The believer has called on the name of the Lord" (Mays, 2006, 8).

While this point obviously applies to one who mourns, it also has a lesson for pastors and church members. When you are responding to a newly bereaved person or family, knowing what to say and how to say it is not easy. You may be called on to pray when you are feeling anxious and not sure what the prayer should contain. During such a time, remember, "in the simple utterance of the name, prayer is made." Take yourself off the hook for thinking that you should be able pray the perfect prayer. Be simple. Call on the name of the Lord, and the prayer is made. If it is hard to know what else to say, perhaps you should express that as well, as part of the address to God:

Lord, we're in shock. Our tongues are silenced. Help us now.

The situation may be so devastating that not much else can or should be prayed in the moment.

Prayer Includes Self-Reflection

Finally, relating to God in conversation includes self-reflection as it occurs in the context of conversing with the divine. Praying "is not merely conversation with the self or communion with the self, except as these happen in the presence of the Lord. God is there for me, known to me, listening to me. All this is actualized in calling on the name" (Mays, 2006, 8–9).

Continuing the story with Anne Lamott, she shows that self-reflection in prayer can be like remembering meaningful past events containing clues to resolving present dilemmas. As the dinner winds down, a bluegrass band begins to play. A woman comes up near the band and begins to dance. Lamott wishes she could do the same, and finally she does, viewing this as a circle of light, like that mentioned by her pastor: "I figured that once I stepped forward into that spotlight, another would appear somewhere near my feet, and if it didn't, at least I'd have had the chance to dance" (1999, 86).

As she sways gently to the music, in a stance of listening within, a memory bubbles up. She recalls a conversation with a priest she had met several years ago, who helped her make an extremely important life-altering decision. This memory is what she needs. She uses the same decision-making process that she used then to decide whether or not to let Sam paraglide—she decides against it (1999, 82–87).

In the ministry of lament, the pastor or church member also can include moments of silence affording the opportunity for self-reflection as part of the address to God. In this case, the self-reflection of the one doing the praying is concerned with the mourners. It may give everyone involved the opportunity to take a deep breath and collect themselves. A memory about God's help in the past may emerge. Most importantly, it affords the opportunity to reflect on the challenge of mourning, as a new psalmist of lament acknowledges the death and seeks to understand it. Then, perhaps words for the prayer will come.

Conclusion

Newly bereaved people going through the first mourning process are beginning to rewrite their life story, including their relationship to God. In the ministry of lament, pastors and church members support this rewriting by affirming mourners as psalmists of lament, in which their mourning finds expression in prayer. Pastors and church members also pray for new mourners. This is one important part of congregational life that helps facilitate the spiritual journey that a new mourner has begun.

CHAPTER 4

It Is OK to Complain to God

In this chapter, the ministry of lament enters grieving territory well beyond the funeral, extending through an indefinite and potentially long time period. Consequently, several mourning processes are related to this long phase of grief, including the second, third, and fourth mourning processes. The present chapter will present the second mourning process, along with the second part of the lament psalms. I will discuss contemporary psalmists of lament, and the chapter will conclude with implications for the ministry of lament.

The Second Phase of Grief

Rando names the second phase of grief the confrontation phase. The primary feature, she says, is "when the mourner confronts the reality of the loss and gradually absorbs what it means." The bereaved person during this time may have a powerful urge to find the lost loved one, pining or yearning for the one who cannot be found. This is neither a one-time experience, nor a short-term experience. Rather, the emphasis is on absorbing the "reality of the loss" gradually. Rando describes this as a learning process in the sense that repeatedly not finding the lost loved one teaches the person to come to grips with the death over time. She gives the example of a man hearing a hilarious joke and picking up the phone to call his brother, only to remember that his brother is dead (1993, 34).

Thomas Attig provides a similar example. Martin and Louise cared for their aged mother, Myra, during her final years. Martin "often catches himself as he is about to call the home to speak to his parents when he arrives and when he occasionally drops her name in conversation as if she were still alive. Such incidents seem momentarily irrational to him, but he quickly shakes them off as painful reminders that Myra no longer lives and that he has much adjusting yet to do" (1996, 27).

Such remembering happens over and over again, according to Rando. "It will take a long time and hundreds, perhaps thousands, of these painful experiences of unfulfilled longing for the deceased before the mourner will be able to transfer to his gut what he knows in his head—that the loved one is really, truly, irrevocably gone" (1993, 34).

Joan Didion shows how powerfully the gut can resist what the head knows—that the loved one is irrevocably gone. As she looks back at the night her husband, author John Dunne, died, she interprets why she needed to spend the night alone:

> I see now that my insistence on spending that first night alone was more complicated than it seemed, a primitive instinct. Of course I knew John was dead. Of course I had already delivered the definitive news to his brother and to my brother and to Quintana's [her daughter's] husband. *The New York Times* knew. The *Los Angeles Times* knew. Yet I was myself in no way prepared to accept this news as final: there was a level on which I believed that what had happened remained reversible. That was why I needed to be alone…After that first night I would not be alone for weeks…but I needed that first night to be alone…I needed to be alone so that he could come back…This was the beginning of my year of magical thinking. (2007, 32–33)

The Second Mourning Process: React to the Separation

The repeated failure to recover the lost loved one is frustrating and results in having to face the loss again and again, if only in the sense of being reminded of the loss. This frustration and facing of the loss is painful. According to Rando, the second mourning process, reacting to the separation, involves allowing the pain of being separated from the lost loved one to be experienced. She emphasizes that the pain of separation may be manifested in every aspect of human functioning, including the psychological, behavioral, social, and physical (1993, 47).

If something is painful, people naturally want to mitigate the pain, that is, alleviate it, or at least find ways to make it less severe. Because the second mourning process involves experiencing the pain of separation, finding ways of mitigating this pain is part of mourning. Psychologists have listed many psychological ways bereaved people mitigate pain, such as avoiding reminders of the deceased (Rando, 1993, 47).

Sometimes, mourners experience extreme ways of mitigating the pain, such as hallucination of the lost loved one, in which the loved one is found temporarily. Several years ago, I visited a church member who had lost her husband three years earlier. She told me about a hallucinatory experience she had had not too long after the funeral, when she was beginning to miss her husband severely. She was sitting in her living room watching television, when her dead husband entered the room from the adjoining hallway, walked across the room in front of her, and then disappeared. He was dressed in his bathrobe, which she recognized as the one he had worn for several years before his death. As a result of this experience, she feared that she was going insane. She confided in another church member, a longtime friend whom she trusted and who had lost a child many years earlier, seeking some wisdom about this experience. The friend reassured her that she was not going insane, and she shared that she had experienced something similar with her deceased child.

In the second part of this mourning process, Rando becomes more specific about the pain that must be experienced as the person reacts to the separation from the deceased. She focuses on painful emotions being experienced and how to deal with them. She suggests that mourners need to cope with the array of responses being experienced, but in ways that help bring a sense of control. This may include such things as identifying and labeling the various emotions being experienced, as well as distinguishing between the different kinds of emotions being experienced. Is guilt or shame taking center stage? Is it anger or fear? This part of mourning also includes finding comfortable and appropriate ways of expressing the emotions being experienced (1993, 47–48).

Finally, Rando points out that mourners react to secondary losses, as well as to the initial loss due to death. The last part of recognizing the loss involves identifying secondary losses and experiencing the pain of separation they bring. Some kinds of secondary loss that Rando cites are roles filled by the deceased, needs previously filled by the deceased that are going unmet, hopes, wishes, and dreams associated with the deceased, and the mourner's worldview that has to change in light of the death or that has been violated because of it (1993, 48).

Joan Didion's "magical thinking" offers a good example of a secondary loss being experienced. The death occurred on December 30, 2003. During late February or early March 2004, she realized that she needed to give John's clothes away. She had helped family members do this when each parent died, and now her husband's clothes needed to be given away. As she started sorting, she began connecting some of his clothes with things they had done together for years, such as his sweatshirts and T-shirts reminding her of early morning walks they took together in Central Park. The clothes served as a reminder of that specific secondary loss, the walks they never could take together again (2007, 36).

Experiencing secondary losses is part of the second mourning process, because they, too, bring the pain of separation needed to teach the grieving person that the death is irreversible. At a certain point, Didion reached a limit to the clothes she could allow herself to pack:

> I was not yet prepared to address the suits and shirts and jackets, but I thought I could handle what remained of the shoes, a start.
> I stopped at the door to the room.
> I could not give away the rest of his shoes.
> I stood there for a moment, then realized why: he would need shoes if he was to return.
> The recognition of this thought by no means eradicated the thought.
> I have still not tried to determine (say, by giving away the shoes) if the thought has lost its power. (2007, 37)

Rewriting a bereaved life story can take many twists and turns, as the grieving person slowly learns at gut level that the death of the person so longed for is irreversible. The story includes instances of experiencing the pain of separation, finding ways of mitigating the pain, and learning appropriate ways of expressing and coping with painful emotions. It also includes discovering the many areas of life affected by the pain of separation, including the spiritual life.

The Second Part of the Lament Psalms: The Complaint

As we saw in chapter 2, the second part of the lament psalms is the complaint. Bernhard Anderson finds that individual and communal complaints follow the address to God and can be about many different types of distress (2000, 61).

Participants in a congregation may well recognize that some church members make complaining a way of life in the church. Surely, then, complaining to God should not be encouraged! No, the complaint in the lament psalms is different. It involves being straightforward with God during a difficult time, not being a chronic complainer to God or to church members and pastors.

Dictionaries tell us that a complaint is an expression of grief, dissatisfaction, pain, or suffering. It can be a grievance involving an accusation. A complaint can be a formal charge brought against someone, as in a court of law. The person complaining has been wronged, oppressed, or caused to suffer. An injustice has occurred, and the person wants it redressed, or set right. Consider, for instance, Psalm 54. Following the address to God in verses 1–2, in which the psalmist asks to be saved, vindicated, and heard, the psalmist makes the complaint in verse 3:

> For the insolent have risen against me,
>> the ruthless seek my life;
> they do not set God before them.

In this complaint, the psalmist expresses a grievance against certain people characterized as insolent, ruthless, and godless people who are threatening the psalmist's life.

In addition to complaints about others, typically described as enemies or foes, some lament psalms contain a personal complaint, in the sense of a lament vividly expressing the psalmist's personal suffering. Still others contain a complaint against God.

The Complaint against God

In the lament psalms, the complaint against God often takes the form of a question, explains Patrick Miller. In these questions, "God's attitudes and actions toward the praying one are questioned and challenged" (1994, 79).

Consider the following examples:

Psalm 13:1
How long, O Lord? Will you forget me forever?

Psalm 44:24
Why do you hide your face?
    Why do you forget our affliction and oppression?

Psalm 77:7–9
"Will the Lord spurn forever,
    and never again be favorable?
Has his steadfast love ceased forever?
    Are his promises at an end for all time?
Has God forgotten to be gracious?
    Has he in anger shut up his compassion?

Miller highlights the fact that these sorts of questions in the lament psalms are protests, not merely requests for information. The complaints against God involve poetic ways of expressing the utterly fundamental and perennial questioning that may race into the mind in the midst of profound loss:

> When one is in distress and trouble, the questions that always come roaring to the forefront of the mind and heart—and here articulated in prayer—are '*Why* is this happening?' or, to God, '*Why* are you doing this (letting this happen, etc.)?' and the complaining query, '*When* is this going to end?' or '*How long* do I have to endure this suffering?' The complaint to God in these prayers thus gives voice to the most fundamental of human questions when life is threatened and falls apart. (1994, 72)

Another way complaints against God are expressed, says Miller, is when the psalmist quotes what someone else has said. The other person, or group, may be questioning God's involvement in, or concern for, the psalmist's predicament. In one example, Miller cites Psalm 3:1–2:

> O Lord, how many are my foes!
>   Many are rising against me;
> many are saying to me,
>   "There is no help for you in God."

While this is an explicit complaint about enemies, it also is an implicit complaint against God, because the quoted words of the foes verbalize the "fear that the psalmist has in light of the affliction and oppression encountered," the fear being that God, indeed, will not help (1994, 73).

The psalmists express other complaints against God as statements directed toward God in the form of assertions or petitions. They may "refer either to God's hiding the face, forgetting, abandoning, being far off, rejecting, and casting off or to the praying one being shamed, taunted, reproached, and mocked, acts that also are directed against God" (Miller, 1994, 75).

Finally, another emphasis involves "expressions of shame, the humiliation of taunts and mockery," writes Miller, citing Psalm 39:9–10. In the second half of verse 8, the psalmist makes a request to God, "Do not make me the scorn of the fool." Then, in verses 9–10, the psalmist complains:

I am silent; I do not open my mouth,
    for it is you who have done it.
Remove your stroke from me;
    I am worn down by the blows of your hand.

Miller says that "it is precisely because of what God has done that the psalmist fears the scorn...of the fool." God is the cause of the psalmist's misery in this complaint (1994, 77).

The Personal Complaint

In the personal complaint, an individual laments about the psalmist's personal condition often expressed in vivid poetic imagery, such as death being imminent. Such an example is Psalm 88:3–6:

For my soul is full of troubles,
    and my life draws near to Sheol.
I am counted among those who go down to the Pit;
    I am like those who have no help,
like those forsaken among the dead,
    like the slain that lie in the grave,
like those whom you remember no more,
    for they are cut off from your hand.
You have put me in the depths of the Pit,
    in the regions dark and deep.

The psalmist may express loneliness, alienation, physical weariness, emotional exhaustion, sickness, or some other personal anguish having to do with physical, mental, or spiritual distress (Miller, 1994, 79–80). Psalm 102:3–11 contains such a powerful complaint that it seems to contain all of these types of suffering:

> For my days pass away like smoke,
>> and my bones burn like a furnace.
> My heart is stricken and withered like grass;
>> I am too wasted to eat my bread.
> Because of my loud groaning
>> my bones cling to my skin.
> I am like an owl of the wilderness,
>> like a little owl of the waste places.
> I lie awake;
>> I am like a lonely bird on the housetop.
> All day long my enemies taunt me;
>> those who deride me use my name for a curse.
> For I eat ashes like bread,
>> and mingle tears with my drink,
> because of your indignation and anger;
>> for you have lifted me up and thrown me aside.
> My days are like an evening shadow;
>> I wither away like grass.

William Brown lifts up the powerful water imagery often used in personal complaints having to do with grief. One use of water images involves an abundance of tears (2002, 118).

Consider Psalm 6:6–7, as an example:

> I am weary with my moaning;
>> every night I flood my bed with tears;
>> I drench my couch with my weeping.
> My eyes waste away because of grief;
>> they grow weak because of all my foes.

Another psalm, 22:14–15, contains water imagery used in staggeringly different ways, from the psalmist's self being dissolved and poured out, to the opposite condition of the psalmist's mouth being dried up. Used in conjunction with another image, melted wax, this shows what Brown calls the formlessness of grief:

> I am poured out like water,
>   and all my bones are out of joint;
> my heart is like wax;
>   it is melted within my breast;
> my mouth is dried up like a potsherd,
>   and my tongue sticks to my jaws;
>   you lay me in the dust of death.

Brown writes, "Wasted with grief, the psalmist enters a state of utter dissolution...As spilled water and melted wax exemplify fluidity, so the psalmist's life ebbs away. Such mixed imagery imbues grief with formlessness. As death approaches, the structures that support and define life dissolve" (2002, 121).

The Complaint about Enemies

Miller lists the third aspect of the complaint as about other people who direct hostility, oppression, and affliction toward the psalmist. These other people often are called enemies, foes, or evildoers (1994, 81–82). Psalm 69:19–21, is an example:

> You know the insults I receive,
>   and my shame and dishonor;
>   my foes are all known to you.
> Insults have broken my heart,
>   so that I am in despair.
> I looked for pity, but there was none;
>   and for comforters, but I found none.
> They gave me poison for food,
>   and for my thirst they gave me vinegar to drink.

Brown identifies a variety of animal metaphors that the psalmist uses to describe the enemies and their destructive effects. Psalm 57:4 features the lion:

> I lie down among lions
>> that greedily devour human prey;
> their teeth are spears and arrows,
>> their tongues sharp swords.

Another deadly species describing the enemy is the serpent, found, for instance, in Psalm 58:3–5:

> The wicked go astray from the womb;
>> they err from their birth speaking lies.
> They have venom like the venom of a serpent,
>> like the deaf adder that stops its ear,
> so that it does not hear the voice of charmers
>> or of the cunning enchanter.

The third animal is the scavenger dog. An example is Psalm 22:16a:

> For dogs are all around me;
>> a company of evildoers encircles me.

Psalmists also use other animals, such as bulls, calves, and even mythological beasts. Brown concludes: "Animal imagery serves to label and, in turn, dehumanize the enemies of God, of Israel, and of the righteous individual" (2002, 135–144).

The Complaint of Contemporary Psalmists of Lament

Mourners, contemporary psalmists of lament, move beyond the address to God when they are ready to write the second part of their lament psalm, the complaint. The pain of separation associated with recognizing the loss, the second mourning process, provides the content informing the complaint, whether it is against God, about enemies, or a lament of personal misery.

A Contemporary Complaint against God

Joan Didion experienced a powerful urge to find her dead husband, John, during her year of magical thinking. At times, her intense frustration at not succeeding in getting him back seems palpable. Her pain at remaining separated from her husband leads to her complaint against God. For certain reasons, the memorial service for her husband was delayed for approximately three months from the time of his death. Didion prefaces her complaint by listing what was done at the memorial service (2007, 42–43):

> We had a Gregorian chant, for John.
>
> Quintana [her daughter] asked that the chant be in Latin. John too would have asked that.
>
> We had a single soaring trumpet.
>
> We had a Catholic priest and an Episcopal priest.
>
> Calvin Trillin spoke. David Halberstam spoke… Quintana, still weak but her voice steady, standing in a black dress in the same cathedral where she had eight months before been married, read a poem she had written to her father.
>
> I had done it. I had acknowledged that he was dead. I had done this in as public a way as I could conceive.

Next, the scene shifts to two or three months after the funeral, around six months after the death. During a dinner conversation about faith, she unexpectedly experiences hostility toward what is being said:

> Yet my thinking on this point remained suspiciously fluid [acknowledging John's death]. At dinner in the late spring or early summer I happened to meet a prominent academic theologian. Someone at the table raised a question about faith. The theologian spoke of ritual itself being a form of faith. My reaction was unexpressed but negative, vehement, excessive even to me.

Didion then remembers the thought she had that lead to her negative reaction:

Later I realized that my immediate thought had been: *But I did the ritual. I did it all.* I did St. John the divine, I did the chant in Latin, I did the Catholic priest and the Episcopal priest, I did "For a thousand years in thy sight are but as yesterday when it is past" and I did *"in paradisum deducant angeli."* And it still didn't bring him back.

If ever a complaint expressed the pain of intense frustration, this has to be it. But it is more than just complaining. Seen as a contemporary psalmist of lament, Didion is making a complaint against God. Implicitly, she is saying something like this:

> *God, if ritual is a form of faith, it doesn't work!*
> *I did everything I was supposed to do—in good faith.*
> *Why did you not do your part?*
> *Why are you leaving me in this awful state?*

Didion is not being impious or inappropriate when she complains about faith and ritual in her book. Her spirituality is genuine and appropriate, as the biblical psalmists of lament show.

A Contemporary Complaint about Enemies

In a book on suicide, Edwin Shneidman included a chapter on his psychotherapeutic care for the bereaved after a traumatic death. One case was about a married couple whose nineteen-year-old daughter had been stabbed to death in a government building one year earlier. The murderer was never caught. The parents were shattered, but after a year they were coping reasonably well.

The second mourning process still was a reality. They continued yearning for their daughter, and the mother reported sometimes mistaking a girl in the neighborhood for her daughter. She also talked to Shneidman about her pain: "There are times when the pain is still there. It's hard to describe it, it's just there, feeling of pain. I guess it's part of sorrow" (1993, 171).

The mother complained about two enemies. The first one was, quite naturally, the murderer: "At the time I wanted the murderer caught and killed. Now I would just like him stopped, but I don't want him killed." The second enemy was an unknown government worker who should have stopped the killing:

> Somebody here helped, and he must know. Whoever it is; who helped, did his part in getting her killed. By not patrolling the building, by not doing—a sin of omission is just as big as a big sin of commission. I mean they knew darn well that the building was not safe (1993, 172).

Some pastors and church members could feel obligated to short-circuit the woman's mourning, insisting that forgiveness should enable her to have no more enemies immediately. However, this would be a false use of forgiveness, because it would just be a way of saying "let go and move on right now" cloaked in religion. Instead, the psalmists of lament show that mourners are to bring their real thoughts and feelings before the God who encourages them to do so, and who listens and responds. Only then will real forgiveness emerge. It is more helpful for pastors and church members to see the woman as a contemporary psalmist of lament who has an implicit complaint against enemies:

> *God, my Lord, evil and sinful people*
> *torture me and my husband by their hiddenness.*
> *Having killed our daughter,*
> *They slither in the shadows, avoiding justice.*
> *But, they must be caught!*

A Contemporary Personal Lament

A fellow pastor told about a member who became dissatisfied with her positon as church organist. One Sunday after worship the church organist requested to speak with the pastor in his office. She told him that she was rather unhappy with the organist position and that she was struggling mightily with depression. Sometimes she could not function for days at a time, which doubly hurt, because she was a perfectionist who needed the time. The pastor successfully referred her to a psychotherapist who was able to help her. In her case, growing far more attentive to her emotional life made a big difference.

Several months later, she again sat in the pastor's office and shared some of her story. The depressive episodes had begun around five years ago, before the present pastor had come to the church. At that time, she was nine months pregnant, but suffered a stillbirth. The baby was born dead because the umbilical cord wound around the baby's neck, choking the baby to death. Her perfectionism, her depression, and her dissatisfaction with her church work gradually had developed into a cover-up for the grief and mourning she had avoided for five years.

Seen as a contemporary psalmist of lament, she had not gotten past the address to God at the time of the death. Now, however, she had begun longing for her lost child and looking with envy at other parents and their small children. Her pain was increasing as she longed for her child, and she was beginning to wrestle with guilt and shame over what had happened. It really was time for her to move to the second part of her lament psalm, the complaint. In her case, it could be a personal lament:

> *My passion, God, has been to pursue avoidance,*
> *while my dead child lay in the grave.*
> *I feel so guilty even though I could not help what happened.*
> *I cry now for my child, but inside I feel dried up.*

The Ministry of Lament to Those Who Complain

The biblical image of the shepherd and the sheep has been central for pastoral care and counseling. However, the second part of the lament psalms, the complaint, challenges this imagery. Psalm 44 is a good example. This psalmist does not see God as a good shepherd leading people beside still waters. Instead, God becomes an untrustworthy leader abandoning the army to slaughter. After a positive address to God, the psalmist begins a long complaint against God in which God rejects the army and even abases the soldiers, belittling and demeaning them, and finally even abandoning them to be killed in verse 11:

> You have made us like sheep for slaughter,
>   and have scattered us among the nations.

Later in the psalm, the psalmist returns to this image of God making us like sheep for slaughter. After acknowledging the fruitlessness of turning away from God, the psalmist blames God for their unfortunate state in verse 22:

> Because of you we are being killed all day long,
>   and accounted as sheep for the slaughter.

This is the verse on which Paul draws in Romans 8:36:

> As it is written,
> "For your sake we are being killed all day long;
>   we are accounted as sheep to be slaughtered."

Right in the midst of his famous passage on nothing being able to separate believers from the love of God in Christ, read in many funerals, Paul inserts this devastating complaint against God, that we are counted as sheep to be slaughtered (Rom. 8:36). The complaint is a challenge to pastors and church members who practice the ministry of lament with bereaved people. One who is experiencing and expressing the pain of grief may complain about God, or may lament personal or family pain. The person also may complain about enemies, who may be innocent professionals with whom the grieving person has to conduct business. Enemies also may be friends who no longer want to socialize with the bereaved person following the death of the loved one. Finally, the mourner may complain about those who practice the ministry of lament, the people who comprise the church. The complaint may be against you. Didion's reaction to the statement of the theologian following the memorial service, discussed above, makes this point, though it ultimately is a complaint against God.

In such a time, those in the ministry of lament must remember that the lament psalms are prayers. God listens to all the complaints and does not discourage them. You, too, should listen and not discourage them. Only then can you have hope for a confession of trust to follow.

Conclusion: What about the Death and Hate Imagery?

Rewriting a bereaved life story is not easy. The second mourning process, react to the separation, boldly challenges those who grieve, including pastors and church members, to face the pain that emerges with loss; and it requires contemporary psalmists of lament to include the complaint in their psalm.

The complaint in the lament psalms is poetry. It raises the most profound questions, "why" and "how long," by poetically complaining against God. It articulates the most profound expressions of individual and communal suffering through personal laments. It gives voice to the most profound accusations against others that human beings can imagine. It reveals the strongest and ugliest feelings and thoughts that can exist in human hearts and minds, what people want most to hide.

Paradoxically, this expression is necessary for new life to emerge. One does not get to resurrection except through crucifixion. This leads to the next chapter, involving the confession of trust and the next mourning process.

CHAPTER 5

Can God Be Trusted?

After the last chapter, which focused on experiencing the pain of grief and complaining to God, this chapter may come as a relief. Bereavement is about more than experiencing and expressing the pain of sorrow. The image of rewriting a life story conveys that grief encompasses many different aspects of life. Similarly, a grieving person's spiritual life is more comprehensive than the complaint conveys by itself. The lament psalms contain spiritual heights as well as the depths. This chapter brings the third mourning process into dialogue with the next part of the lament psalms, and these will be brought to bear on contemporary psalmists of lament. Finally, I will draw implications for the ministry of lament.

The Third Mourning Process: Recollect and Reexperience the Deceased and the Relationship

In the third mourning process, the mourner is becoming able to sustain a focus on remembering the deceased person and the relationship with that person before the person died. Rando calls the third mourning process recollect and reexperience the deceased and the relationship (1993, 48).

Because the dead person is absent, no longer present physically, the mourner must learn new ways of relating to others, to the world, to the deceased, and even to the mourner's own self. The third mourning process enables the mourner to take a step in this direction. It involves loosening and untying the bonds the person has with the deceased, freeing the person to move toward learning new ways of relating in these areas of life. This loosening and untying is not easy. It is understandable, says Rando, that a grieving person may resist turning attention toward this needed mourning process and, accordingly, that it will take time. "It is only over time, when it becomes increasingly apparent that holding on is useless and even harmful, that the mourner starts to let go of old attachments and ultimately develop new ones" (1993, 49).

Making this sort of change to live without the physical presence of the deceased does not mean that the mourner stops relating to the deceased family member or friend. In fact, engaging in the third mourning process actually helps the mourner begin relating to the deceased in ways that will be ongoing throughout life. You can see this in the story of one mourner, a contemporary psalmist of lament, discussed later in the chapter.

According to Rando, "The mourner is tied to the deceased by thousands of attachment bonds." These bonds are simply the various aspects of the relationship that brought the two together and held them together in relationship over time. Some of these attachment bonds are "needs for that special person, the unique relationship, and the gratification and meaning they provided; feelings, thoughts, behavior and interaction patterns, hopes, wishes, fantasies, and dreams about that person and the mutual relationship; and a host of assumptions, expectations, and beliefs" (1993, 49).

Obviously, the possible ties helping to maintain the relationship cover a wide range, such as those associated with marriage, all sorts of other family relationships, and friendships. It stands to reason that when the person dies, all of the "attachment bonds" do not just go away. They remain very much alive in the mourner, continuing to be a strong influence in the mourner's self-understanding and view of the world that were developed in the context of the relationship with the deceased. It also stands to reason that bonds must begin to be loosened and untied in accord with the reality that the loved one no longer is present in the flesh. Again, this goes hand-in-hand with learning to relate to the deceased in a new way.

The third mourning process has two main features that describe how the needed loosening and untying of bonds happens. The first one involves recollecting, and it is called "review and remember realistically." The second part involves reexperiencing, and it is called "revive and reexperience the feelings." Rando says that she divided the third mourning process into these two parts to make the discussion easier. In reality, however, the two are "not so amenable to dissection" (1993, 48–50, 414–423).

Reviewing and Remembering Realistically

As a pastor, I have had many occasions to visit the home of an individual or family of someone who has just died. Sometimes friends will be present, or relatives will have arrived from out of town. One common part of the conversation involves telling stories about the deceased from weeks, months, or years ago. These stories may bring laughter or sadness, but they are always positive, never critical of the lost loved one. This tends to be true even when the relationship between the deceased and survivors has been destructive and painful. While mourners may allude to the negative situation, such as "her drinking became too much for me during the past two years," the recollections most often turn to better times. Honoring the recently dead involves idealizing, accentuating the positive and turning a blind eye to the negative. The person was kind, funny, gentle; never harsh, rude, verbally abusive.

This reaction comes at the beginning of grief. A time comes when the recollecting or the remembering must move from being idealistic to realistic. The timing may be different for every bereaved person. Remembering and the stories that memories conjure up now need to be expanded to include the bereaved person's real experience, including the positive, ambivalent, and negative things remembered about the deceased person and the relationship with that person. According to Rando, "In healthy mourning, the deceased must be remembered realistically. This means that *all* aspects of the person and the mutual relationship must be recalled—all of the positives, negatives, and neutrals" (1993, 49).

In addition to being realistic, the mourner needs to take seriously another word, *review*. Mourners will need many times of remembering if salient aspects of the relationship helpful to mourning are to be recalled, requiring an intentional evaluation, or review, of the relationship as it unfolded over time. "The mourner must repeatedly review the entire relationship, the expectations and needs that initially formed it, its ups and downs, its course and development, its crises and joys—all elements of it throughout the years" (Rando, 1993, 49).

Reviving and Reexperiencing the Feelings

Rando writes that feelings, however positive, negative, or ambivalent, connect human beings in relationship. "Deep feelings, like a psychological electromagnetic current, provide the ongoing magnetism between us and our loved ones" Feelings, then, must be revived and reexperienced, as part of remembering and reviewing the deceased and the relationship with the deceased. Put simply, the feelings "must be felt." Allowing emotion to be part of recollecting has the effect of lessening the power of the emotion to play its role of "magnetism" (1993, 421).

Another image Rando uses to convey the loosening of the relational bonds is dimming the lights with a dimmer switch. "The dimmer switch is turned down as the mourner expends his emotions, and the lights dim naturally as a consequence of the reduced affect caused by readjustments to the absence of the deceased...they are softer, less fiery—more warm, less intense" (1993, 421–422).

Two Trajectories

At this point, two different yet interrelated trajectories of mourning come into focus. On the one hand, recollecting and reexperiencing the deceased and the relationship enables a grieving person to begin changing the relationship in the sense of having the "lights dim," allowing the mourner to make progress toward living in a healthy manner without the deceased being physically present. On the other hand, this mourning process enables one who mourns to make an important step forward in developing a new kind of relationship with the one who died. It is a relationship "of memory and not of presence" (Rando, 1993, 422).

The Third Part of the Lament Psalms:
The Confession of Trust

Bernhard Anderson labels the third part of the lament psalms "the confession of trust." It involves a shift from the complaint to proclaiming trust in God (2000, 61). An example is Psalm 38:15. The complaint is extensive. The psalmist has been rebuked by God and is wounded, spent, and crushed. Friends and neighbors distance themselves. Enemies plan treachery. Then, in verse 15, the psalmist shifts gears, expressing the confession of trust:

> But it is for you, O Lord, that I wait;
> it is you, O Lord my God, who will answer.

Claus Westermann affirms that the confession of trust follows the complaint. However, he notes that sometimes it comes after the fourth part of the lament psalms, the petition (1965, 57).

Anderson says that the confession of trust involves having confidence in God. "This is an expression of confidence in God in spite of the problematic situation." Trust understood in terms of confidence indicates that the psalmist is viewing God as reliable, or worthy of trust. The psalmist can rely on God in spite of the situation about which the psalmist has just complained even if the complaint is against God. This confidence in God's reliability can be seen in the way the psalmist makes the transition from the complaint to the confession of trust. As Anderson points out, the psalmist typically introduces the confession of trust with words such as "but" or "nevertheless" (2000, 61). Here are some examples:

Psalm 3:3
But you, O Lord, are a shield around me,
    my glory, and the one who lifts up my head.

Psalm 31:14
But I trust in you, O Lord;
    I say, "You are my God."

Psalm 102:12
But you, O Lord, are enthroned forever;
    your name endures to all generations.

The word *confession* in the confession of trust also is important. The psalmist is intentionally acknowledging this trust in God. Articulating confidence in God's reliability is an explicit part of the prayer in the lament psalms. Psalm 55:16–19, for instance, contains a confession of trust following a complaint about enemies and especially the betrayal of a friend:

But I call upon God,
    and the Lord will save me.
Evening and morning and at noon
    I utter my complaint and moan,
    and he will hear my voice.
He will redeem me unharmed
    from the battle that I wage,
    for many are arrayed against me.
God, who is enthroned from of old,
    will hear, and will humble them—
because they do not change,
    and do not fear God.

The psalmist trusts God for a purpose. The psalmist is not just expressing trust in general, but instead is expressing confidence that God will help, or will respond to the psalmist's requests to make the situation right. As Psalm 55 promises, God will "save me," will "hear my voice," will "redeem me unharmed from the battle I wage."

Ways of Expressing Trust

Patrick Miller writes that the psalmists of lament tend to express their confessions of trust in several ways:

First Type. In the first type, the psalmist makes a statement about God. According to Miller, in this statement, "some characteristic or quality or way of God's being and doing is lifted up in relation to the psalmist" (1994, 127). The divine quality or action on which the psalmist focuses may have to do with the very thing the psalmist is seeking. For instance, in Psalm 54:3, the complaint is about insolent, ruthless people who seek the psalmist's life. Verse 4 contains the confession of trust in which the psalmist calls God a helper who will uphold the psalmist's life:

> But surely, God is my helper;
> the LORD is the upholder of my life.

Psalmists may use many images to convey confidence in God's help, such as God being the psalmist's shield or rock. They may include expressions of confidence in God's salvation and references to past deliverance. For example, in Psalm 74 the psalmist complains against God, but then expresses trust in verse 12:

> Yet God my King is from of old,
> working salvation in the earth.

Finally, the psalmist may express confidence in God's opposition to evil. "Confidence in God's opposition to the wicked and evil is expressed in these prayers, as well as the conviction of God's protection against the forces of wickedness and oppression and the enemies of the suppliant" (Miller, 1994, 127).

Second Type. The second way that the psalmists of lament tend to express their confessions of trust, says Miller, is by making a "straightforward confession of trust in God." In this case, the focus is on the psalmist who is praying (1994, 127). Psalm 59 provides a helpful comparison of both types. The psalmist complains about enemies who are bloodthirsty and like howling dogs. Then, in verses 8–10, the psalmist expresses confidence in God. Verse 8 is the first type of expressing trust, in which the psalmist makes a statement about God:

> But you laugh at them, O LORD;
> you hold all the nations in derision.

In verses 9–10, the psalmist shifts to the second type. Now, the focus is on the psalmist, who will watch for God, who will be loved by God, and who will be enabled to look triumphantly on the defeated enemies:

> O my strength, I will watch for you;
> for you, O God, are my fortress.
> My God in his steadfast love will meet me;
> my God will let me look in triumph on my enemies.

Finally, Miller puts the confession of trust in perspective, placing it in the context of the lament psalm as a whole, the psalmist's prayer for help. It shows that the psalmist's prayer is an act of faith. Far from negating the complaint expressed out of despair, it reveals the psalmist to be in a stance of trust toward God throughout the prayer. As Miller writes,

> Whatever despair and anguish may be present in the lament, even in the complaints against God, the expressions of confidence underline what is implicit in the petition: God may be the problem, but God is, even more, the only way out, the one possible help in a situation of helplessness, the solid rock when everything teeters on the verge of destruction or oblivion. (1994, 130)

The Confession of Trust of Contemporary Psalmists of Lament

At first glance, the third mourning process and the confession of trust may not seem to be naturally suited to be in dialogue. In reality, they share much in common.

The psalmist begins the confession of trust with a "but," or a "nevertheless," indicating an important shift from complaint to an expression of confidence in God's reliability. This trust does not mean that all the devastating pain is gone or that the situation has changed at this point. Nonetheless, the confession of trust in the lament psalms is forward looking in the sense that it anticipates divine help for making the situation right so that the psalmist will have the possibility of living fruitfully again in the future.

Similarly, when rewriting a bereaved life story involves the third mourning process, a similar kind of shift takes place, as if an implicit "but" or "nevertheless" introduces recollecting and reexperiencing the deceased and the relationship. The mourner is able to reflect on the life of the deceased for constructive, life-affirming purposes. This is not to say, of course, that no pain is involved, because recollecting and reexperiencing the deceased and the mourner's relationship with the deceased is becoming realistic, in which the mourner must recall negative as well as positive aspects of the person and relationship. Yet this mourning process is forward looking in the sense that it anticipates new possibilities for living in future chapters yet to be written.

In Wendell Berry's novel, *Jayber Crow*, the main character, Jayber Crow, tells about something that surprisingly can be seen as a metaphor showing how meaningful the third mourning process can be. Crow tells about his job as grave digger and church janitor in his little town. He says that the grave digging was hard work, and many times it was sad work, because "as a rule I would be digging and filling the grave of somebody I knew; often it would be the grave of somebody I liked or loved" (2000, 157).

At first, this seems like a rather unpleasant topic, but his reflection leads in a meaningful direction. The physical act of grave digging leads Crow to ponder the mystery of death, especially how the living view the dead and relate to them:

> It was a strange thing to cut out the blocks of sod and then dig my way to the dark layer where the dead lie. I feel a little uneasy in calling them 'the dead,' for I am as mystified as anybody by the transformation

known as death, and the Resurrection is more real to me than most things I have not yet seen. I understand that people's dead bodies are not exactly *them*, and yet as I dug down to where they were, I would be mindful of them, and respectful, and would feel a curious affection for them all. They all had belonged here once, and they were so much more numerous than the living. I thought and thought about them. (2000, 157–8)

In her discussion of the third mourning process, Rando points out that a grieving person may resist reviewing the relationship with a lost loved one for such reasons as avoiding painful memories or avoiding something from the relationship about which the bereaved person feels guilty (1993, 416–17). Jayber Crow, however, shows that, strange though it may seem, digging past the surface of the relationship, into layers of it that you would rather leave alone, may engender a new understanding of how the living relate to their lost loved one, as well as a growing respect and lasting affection for the deceased.

The Confession of Trust

The third mourning process, then, provides the content informing the confession of trust of the mourner, the contemporary psalmist of lament. This marks an important shift in the bereaved person's relationship with God, from complaint to confidence in God's reliability. Recall the confession of trust in Psalm 54:4 above:

But surely, God is my helper;
　　the LORD is the upholder of my life.

In the contemporary confession of trust, the mourner is praying:

God, you are my helper, upholding my life
as I remember my lost loved one
and feel the feelings that come with remembering;

and take the time and energy needed
to review different aspects of our relationship;
and face the parts of the relationship that I wanted to forget.
I trust that with your support and help, God,
this demanding challenge will have meaningful and desirable
   results.

A Confession of Trust after a Loss from Suicide

Frederick Buechner begins his autobiographical book, *Telling Secrets*, this way: "One November morning in 1936 when I was ten years old, my father got up early, put on a pair of gray slacks and a maroon sweater, opened the door to look in briefly on my younger brother and me, who were playing a game in our room, and then went down into the garage where he turned on the engine of the family Chevy and sat down on the running board to wait for the exhaust to kill him" (1991, 7).

The next few pages are gut wrenching. They held no funeral, and neither Buechner, his mother, nor his brother attended the burial. None of them ever talked much about his father with each other, or with others outside the family, because suicide was looked on as "shabby and shameful in those days." Two months after the death, they moved from New Jersey to Bermuda, which enhanced the family's effort to forget rather than remember. Buechner says that after the move he could not even "remember remembering him." Within a year, he forgot what his father looked like except for photographs, what his voice sounded like, and what it was like to be with him. No one talked about how they felt about him when he was alive, or after he died, so "those feelings soon disappeared too and went underground along with the memories...in almost no time at all, it was as if, at least for me, he had never existed" (1991, 8–9).

If feelings and memories can go underground, they also can be dug up. In Buechner's case, such digging seems as gut wrenching as his forgetting. Later in the book, he shares some of what he had dug up in adulthood:

> If somebody had asked me as a little boy of eight or nine, say, what my secrets were, I wonder if I would have thought to list among them a father who at parties drank himself into a self I could hardly recognize as my father, and a mother who in her rage could say such wild and scathing things to him that it made the very earth shake beneath my feet when I heard them, and a two-and-a-half years younger brother who for weeks at a time would refuse to get out of bed because bed, I suspect, was the only place he knew in the whole world where he felt safe (1991, 73).

It could seem as if forgetting is preferable to remembering and feeling, at least where misery is involved. Yet remembering and feeling ultimately made it possible for Buechner to do something he could not possibly have done otherwise. He began relating to his father differently after several decades. He had gone to see a psychotherapist. "A lot of what she did was not just to help me remember forgotten parts of my childhood and to recapture some of the feelings connected with them, which I had discovered as a child that I would do well to forget, but also to suggest certain techniques for accomplishing that." (In one technique, she would have Buechner write about his childhood days using his left hand. This was awkward because he was right handed, but it had the desired effect. One day she asked him to write out a dialogue with his father when he returned home from the session with her (1991, 98).

In a portion of the dialogue, Buechner asks his father if he remembers the last time they saw each other. He does remember. Then, he asks his father if he was sad, if he was scared, and if he knew what he was going to do. His father replies that he had to do it, because he had no way out. Then Buechner asks his father a question that many survivors of suicide will recognize:

> CHILD: Could I have stopped you, Daddy? If I'd told you I loved you? If I told you how I needed you?

FATHER: No nobody could. I was lost so badly.

Next, Buechner asks if this really is his father:

CHILD: Is this really you I'm talking to? I can't see your face. I've forgotten your voice, your smell.

FATHER: I remember you. I was proud of you. I wanted you to like me.

Then, Buechner tells his father how he feels:

CHILD: I've been so worried. I've been so scared ever since.

FATHER: Don't be. There is nothing to worry about. That is the secret I never knew, but I know it now.

Finally, Buechner tells his father that he loves him and says goodbye (1991, 99–100).

On the one hand, Buechner found a better way than ever before to tell his father goodbye. On the other hand, he began developing a sense of relating to his father in a new way. In his reflection on this imaginative dialogue, Buechner acknowledges that the left handed exercise helped him dredge up things out of himself. Yet he also acknowledges his sense that he really was talking to his father, which he conveys with this quote: "'There are more things in heaven and earth, Horatio,/Than are dreamt of in your philosophy.'—in some sense it really was my father I was talking to. Who knows? Who can say for sure either way?" (1991, 100).

As a survivor of suicide, Buechner has allowed mourning to be part of the ebb and flow of his life journey. His metaphorical grave digging, his remembering and feeling, show that he can be seen as a contemporary psalmist of lament who expresses a confession of trust implicitly. It might go something like this:

Lord God, your strong support makes it possible for me to remember my father.
You encourage me when I have to face what I wanted to forget.

You continue to be with me when I feel some very painful
feelings,
especially those that come with remembering suicide.
Your help, God, enables me to mourn my loss
and even find meaning in relating to my father.

Implications for the Ministry of Lament

A pastor, a church member, or small group of church members may have different responses when they listen to the confession of trust of a bereaved person, which involves talking about the deceased and the mourner's relationship to the deceased while the person still was alive. One kind of response might be to think that the mourner is dwelling too much on the past, and, instead, the mourner should focus more on the future. But this flies in the face of the confession of trust. Instead, a better response is to honor the person's engagement in the third mourning process, in the recognition that significant rewriting is taking place. It is a step toward relating to others, the world, and the self fruitfully and realistically in the future, while still maintaining an appropriate relationship to the deceased. This better response is congruent with viewing the bereaved person's mourning as containing an implicit shift in relating to God, from complaint to the confession of trust. In some instances a bereaved person may not recognize the spiritual shift that has taken place until it is pointed out.

Another response may be reflected in worship or prayer or reflection on scripture. It is the affirmation that explicitly articulating confidence in God's reliability is appropriate in relation to the third mourning process. It is expressing trust in God's help for reviewing the past relationship with the deceased realistically and having an expectation that something positive will come of it.

An unhelpful response would be to view expressions of trusting in God's help to be a cover-up for negative feelings being harbored toward God because of the death or the pain of grief. Because the mourners, as well as the pastor and congregation, have freedom to express their complaints, the confession of trust can be affirmed as genuine and appropriate.

A final response involves respecting the kind of experience that Buechner had in the story above. In addition to his psychological awareness regarding his imaginative conversation with his dead father, he also had the sense that he really was talking to his father. Rather than brushing such experiences aside, those who practice the ministry of lament must remember the grave digging metaphor. Something powerful comes from digging into a past relationship. It is the rudimentary beginning of developing and maintaining a relationship with the deceased for the rest of life, as well as preparation for relating to others, the world, and the self anew.

Conclusion

Remembering and feeling are common everyday human experiences. Yet in the context of mourning, they assume extraordinary importance. How important it is to review the relationship with a lost loved one for the purpose of becoming free to move into the present without the physical presence of the deceased, while at the same time coming to establish an appropriate ongoing relationship with the deceased without that person's physical presence. Likewise, how important it is spiritually to move from complaint to a confession of trust. As a contemporary psalmist of lament, the mourner does indeed confess trust, preparing for more rewriting yet to come.

CHAPTER 6

Asking God for Help

Bereaved people, like all human beings, sometimes must wrestle with changing some aspect of their life that is no longer viable. That old part of life may be treasured, but, at the same time, healthy living in the present requires change. The mourning process introduced in the present chapter addresses this issue. Because such change is difficult, many people ask God for help. This appeal to God is called the petition, which is the part of the lament psalms I will present following discussion of the mourning process. Next, I will bring the two into dialogue in the section on the contemporary psalmist of lament. Finally, I will draw implications for the ministry of lament.

The Fourth Mourning Process:
Relinquish the Old Attachments to the Deceased and the Old Assumptive World

Recall from the last chapter that the third mourning process contains two trajectories. In one of them, remembering realistically is in the service of learning gradually to live in the present without the physical presence of the deceased. Such remembering has the effect of loosening ties, or relational bonds, with the deceased. The fourth mourning process builds on this trajectory by describing the next step past loosening ties. It involves going beyond loosening, all the way to relinquishing particular ties if needed, but not all ties. Rando names this mourning process "relinquish the old attachments to the deceased and the old assumptive world" (1993, 50).

The second trajectory of the third mourning process involves remembering realistically in order to begin establishing a new kind of relationship with the deceased, one based in memory rather than physical presence. The fourth mourning process does not focus on this trajectory directly. Instead, this mourning process is needed to prepare the soil for growing the new relationship with the deceased, which the next chapter will address. Rando actually begins her discussion of the fourth mourning process by discussing the relationship between these two things:

> Before the mourner can transform the previous relationship with the deceased into something more appropriate to the loved one's new status, he must relinquish old attachments to that person. In addition, he must surrender his attachments to his old assumptive world, constructed on the basis of the loved one's existence. (1993, 50)

Relinquishing Attachments to the Deceased

As Rando uses the word, *attachments* essentially is another word meaning the same thing as ties, relational bonds, or connections to the deceased. The notion of relinquishing attachments may raise eyebrows. For instance, if one kind of attachment involves love, it would seem cruel to think that healthy mourning should require giving up that love. At the same time, however, loving connections to the deceased requiring that person's physical presence and interaction with the mourner no longer are possible. In a marriage, for example, sexual intimacy, one significant expression of love, is no longer an option with the now-deceased partner. So, the kinds of attachments Rando addresses are those the mourner needs to give up at some point through a voluntary choice, because the deceased no longer can respond. "The mourner must learn to be without the particular interaction, validation, reinforcement, and role-fulfilling behaviors previously existing in the relationship" (1993, 51).

This also shows that relinquishing an attachment must be taken seriously. In its most generic dictionary definition, relinquish means to give up something. This can happen in different ways and can have slightly different meanings. For example, it can mean releasing your grasp on something, like the steering wheel of a car. Or, it can mean renouncing something, such as an unwanted position in an organization. It can mean yielding to someone's wishes, waiving your rights, or abandoning hope for something.

Consider the situation in which the partner in a household who always managed the finances dies. The other partner has depended on the deceased to fulfill this role for years, but now can depend on no one else to manage the finances. At some point, the mourner must relinquish this tie of dependency to the deceased if the bills are to be paid. The relinquishment can be understood in the sense of the mourner abandoning hope that somehow the situation will work out so that the finances will be managed as they were in the past. In no way can this be construed as meaning that the mourner no longer loves the deceased or breaks all ties.

Another side to this type of situation also exists. According to Rando, sometimes a mourner may not realize that an old tie has been relinquished except in retrospect. "For instance, it may become apparent that the mourner is letting go of her reliance upon the deceased only after she has taken a particular risk on her own." In the example above, the mourner may have visited a financial advisor, hired an accountant, and began learning what is involved in managing stocks and bonds. It could be that, having taken this risk of learning financial management, the mourner realizes in retrospect that the tie of dependency is relinquished. Now, relinquishment may mean that the mourner proudly, if sadly, renounces this tie as something no longer needed (1993, 425).

Finally, Rando discusses some reasons that a mourner may resist relinquishing attachments. The main reason is that the mourner simply does not want to give them up, based on one of many possible motivations:

> She does not want to because she fears that then she will have no connection to the loved one and that to do so means he really is dead. She does not want to because it makes her feel insecure and anxious, and because she cannot imagine life without him. She does not want to because she does not think she can manage to do it and because her ties to the deceased defined parts of herself. She does not want to be different now, but wants to go back to the old world, the old life, the old relationship, and the old self. She does not want to because this was not the way her life was supposed to go. And so on. (1993, 424)

Relinquishing Attachments to the Old Assumptive World

If you own a car and park it on the street when you go into a store, normally you take for granted that it will be there when you return. You have no proof that it has not been stolen while out of your sight. You just assume based on past experience. You would be shocked if it were stolen. People make assumptions about the world, themselves, and their relationships as a matter of course in their daily lives. Requiring a new round of proof for everything taken to be the case, or true, each day would be untenable for living. Rando shows how dealing with assumptions is part of the fourth mourning process.

Rando does not address just random or individual assumptions, however. She addresses what psychotherapists call the assumptive world, understood as "an organized schema containing everything a person assumes to be true about the world and the self on the basis of previous experience." The assumptive world begins developing in infancy and continues throughout life. It affects us greatly, including helping determine our needs, shaping behavior, and forming a lens through which we interpret reality. The assumptive world is a concept in psychotherapy often used to understand trauma, including traumatic death and its effects on survivors (1993, 50).

The assumptive world with which Rando is concerned is the old assumptive world of the mourner. By old, she means the mourner's assumptive world during the time when the deceased loved one was still alive. The death of the loved one may have a powerful impact on the mourner's assumptive world, resulting in the need for its revision in light of the death. Rando points out that for this to happen, old assumptions must be relinquished to make way for new ones (1993, 426).

Global assumptions. Some assumptions are global in the sense of pertaining to "the self, others, life, or the world in general." In some instances, the circumstances surrounding the death of the loved one may violate or assault a global assumption. Rando gives the example of murder. It may shatter an assumption of invulnerability. It may destroy a view of the world as meaningful. It may cause the belief that God protects innocent people to be invalidated (1993, 51).

Ronnie Janoff-Bulman maintains that three fundamental assumptions form the core of the assumptive world:

The world is benevolent
The world is meaningful
The self is worthy. (1992, 6)

Jeffrey Kauffman relates the assumption about benevolence to safety and shows how loss of safety is fundamental in traumatic loss:

> The nature of mortality, sacred and hidden—and, likewise, the guts of animal fear—urges upon self a primary concern with safety. And, in the mortal urgency of traumatic loss, the primary concern for safety, for protection against (traumatizing) violation, is, at the time of traumatic loss and continuing afterward, urgent and radical. (2002, 207)

Kauffman also distinguishes between traumatic and nontraumatic loss of the assumptive world. He says that it is the difference between panic and anxiety. "In traumatic loss there is persistent helplessness panic and annihilation panic, and in nontraumatic loss there is helplessness anxiety and annihilation anxiety more or less persistently" (2002, 207).

Specific assumptions. Other sorts of assumptions have to do with the relationship between the mourner and the deceased in particular. The ties between the mourner and the loved one are represented in the assumptive world. These assumptions are specific in the sense that they are about the loved person's presence and interaction with the mourner while that person was still alive. Rando gives the example, "She will be there for me always" (1993, 51).

Recall the illustration in the previous section about the person who needed to learn how to manage finances following the death of the partner. The tie of dependency on the deceased person also had a counterpart in the assumptive world: "My partner always will take care of me financially." This relieved the person of having to learn financial management. However, just as the old tie must be relinquished, so the related specific assumption also must be relinquished. Obviously, the partner no longer can take care of the mourner financially. Relinquishing the old assumption frees the mourner to embrace a new one: "I am a person capable of caring for myself financially." This assumption is congruent with the practical necessity of actually learning and practicing financial management.

At first, this new assumption may be a possibility entertained in the mourner's imagination. Then, as the person actually learns financial management, it may be embraced as an assumption into which the mourner grows. It becomes part of the mourner's revised assumptive world.

Finally, Rando acknowledges how difficult it may be to relinquish old assumptions:

> Thus, for mourners, as for all human beings, life has been predicated on certain assumptions. Some of the major ones revolve around meaning, security, fairness, control, predictability, and invulnerability. When one or several of these must be reconsidered

after the death of a loved one, the others may become suspect as well. Mourners fear that, like a house of cards, the whole assumptive world will come tumbling down. (1993, 427)

The Fourth Part of the Lament Psalms: The Petition

Anderson describes the fourth part of the lament psalms as the petition. This means that the psalmist makes a serious or urgent request, an appeal, to God. The appeal is for God to intervene in the situation that the psalmist expresses in the psalm and for God to deliver the psalmist from it. He cites Psalm 6:4 as an example:

> Turn, O LORD, save my life;
> deliver me for the sake of your steadfast love.

Anderson also points out that the psalmist sometimes includes grounds, or reasons, supporting the petition. Continuing with Psalm 6, he shows the supporting argument for the petition in verse 5:

> For in death there is no remembrance of you;
> in Sheol who can give you praise?

This verse supplies grounds for God to intervene and deliver the psalmist according to the petition for deliverance. If God wants to be remembered and praised, then God should save the life of the one who will do these things (2000, 61).

Biblical scholars call this part of the psalm the motivational clause, in which the psalmist is trying to motivate God to act on the petition. Walter Brueggemann lists several kinds of motivations found in the lament psalms:

The speaker is *innocent* and so is entitled to help.

The speaker is *guilty*, but repents and seeks forgiveness and restoration.

The speaker recalls God's *goodness to an earlier generation*, which serves as a precedent for God's goodness now. God should do once again what was done in the past.

The speaker is *valued by God* as one who praises. If the speaker is permitted to die, the speaker will cease to praise, and the loss will be Yahweh's.

The speaker finally goes beyond self and appeals to Yahweh to consider *God's own power, prestige, and reputation.* (1984, 55)

Miller believes the petition is at the heart of prayers for help in the scriptures, including lament psalms. He observes that the words *lament* and *complaint* used in relation to these prayers for help may lead to the assumption that the main function of the prayer is to lament or complain. This is not true. Instead, the fundamental purpose involves attempting to obtain God's help. "So the petition or plea is where one discerns the basic intention of the prayer for help." At the same time, however, petitions typically do not tell precisely what is wrong. Is the psalmist physically ill and near death? Or is the difficulty emotional? The entire psalm remains general enough in its poetry to elicit many possible interpretations. According to Miller, this generality, or even stereotyping, is characteristic of the petition in the lament psalms (1994, 86–87).

Different Kinds of Petitions

Because the complaint, the second part of the lament psalms, sets forth a troublesome, painful situation, it makes sense that the petition would have something to do with it. Yet just as there are different kinds of complaints having to do with many varied forms of suffering, so there is not just one petition. Nor do all petitions have some automatic one to one correspondence with the complaint, as if appealing to God for help were mechanical. If two people, for example, have a similar complaint, each of them could have a different petition, both being equally valuable. Even the same person might have a different petition about the same situation on different days. Miller conveys the breadth of petitions in the lament psalms by identifying eleven different types of petition found in them:

1. Seeking God's Attention (1994, 97–99)

Many petitions in the lament psalms involve seeking God's attention. God is asked to hear the psalmist. Some lament psalms even begin in the first verse with the petition for God to hear. In this case, the initial part of the psalm, the address to God, does double duty as both address and petition, an example being Psalm 17:1:

> Hear a just cause, O LORD; attend to my cry;
>   give ear to my prayer from lips free of deceit.

Notice that in addition to the word "hear," the psalmist also uses "attend" and "give ear." Additional imagery in other psalms also is used to seek God's attention, such as wanting God to answer, consider, draw near, or awaken.

2. Petitions and the Complaint (1994, 99–102)

The focus on petitions and complaint is not so much an identification of one kind of petition among others, as it is as emphasis on the interplay between the petition and complaint, particularly complaints against God in personal laments. In some instances, the petition uses imagery similar to that in the complaint, or imagery that closely corresponds to it, such as that in Psalm 3. Verse 2 contains a complaint:

> many are saying to me,
>   "There is no help for you in God."

The first part of verse 7 contains the corresponding petition requesting help from God:

> Rise up, O LORD!
>   Deliver me, O my God!

Miller makes the interesting point that the petition in one psalm may contain the same imagery found in the complaint in another psalm. In other words, different lament psalms may borrow imagery from one another, creating a correspondence between complaints and petitions among different psalms.

3. *Grace and Mercy (1994, 102–3)*

In some petitions, the psalmist asks God to be gracious or merciful. In Psalm 31:9, for example, the psalmist is endangered and afflicted, having adversaries who may hatch a secret plan to ensnare the psalmist. The petition comes in verse 9:

> Be gracious to me, O LORD, for I am in distress;
> my eye wastes away from grief,
> my soul and body also.

According to Miller, the petition for grace and mercy appeals to God's compassion, "to look with favor upon those in trouble, to forgive sins, to help when someone is undone by oppressive forces" (1994, 102).

4. *Salvation, Deliverance, and Help (1994, 103–5)*

According to Miller, the largest number of petitions involves requests for help, conveyed with different imagery, such as deliverance, rescue, salvation, and redemption. An example is Psalm 142:6, which has two petitions. The first line contains an appeal for God's attention, followed by an appeal for God to save in the third line:

> Give heed to my cry,
> for I am brought very low.
> Save me from my persecutors,
> for they are too strong for me.

This second sort of petition, for salvation, may be in response to a great variety of complaints. They may include everything from international threats, to false accusations, oppression of the poor, illness, guilt, or abandonment.

5. *Protection (1994, 105–6)*

In this kind of petition, the psalmist appeals to God for protection from harm. The petition for protection is rooted in the conviction that God is a refuge from many different kinds of distress. For instance, in Psalm 25, the psalmist expresses concern about being shamed in verse 1. Then, in verse 20, the petition addresses this issue:

> O guard my life, and deliver me;
>> do not let me be put to shame, for I take refuge in you.

6. Against the Enemy (1994, 106–8)

Miller cites Psalm 17 as a representative example of the petition against enemies discussed in the complaint. The psalmist is being treated badly by some pitiless and arrogant people. Verses 8–9 contain a petition for protection from the enemies. Then, in verses 13–14 comes the petition against these enemies:

> Rise up, O LORD, confront them, overthrow them!
>> By your sword deliver my life from the wicked,
> from mortals—by your hand, O LORD—
>> from mortals whose portion in life is in this world.
> May their bellies be filled with what you have stored up for them;
>> may their children have more than enough;
>> may they leave something over to their little ones.

This harsh kind of petition cannot be taken at face value as a vindictive outburst, though it manifests powerful negative emotions. Instead, the petition against the enemies is another form of appealing to God for help. "It is only as they are undone that the psalmist can be saved and protected" (Miller, 107).

7. Healing (1994, 108)

The complaint in lament psalms sometimes is cast in the language of sickness, which often can be taken either as a literal illness or metaphorically as some kind of personal disintegration. In Psalm 102, for instance, the psalmist expresses incredible suffering, from aching bones, to a stricken heart, to taunting enemies. The petition for healing comes in verse 24:

"O my God," I say, "do not take me away
   at the mid-point of my life,
you whose years endure
   throughout all generations."

8. Judgment and Vindication (1994, 108–10)

The petition for judgment and vindication is in response to some oppressive accusation being made against the psalmist who needs justice. The way out of the predicament is for "God to sustain the innocence of the petitioner and render the accusers guilty for their oppressive deceit" (108). A good example is Psalm 7. People portrayed as lions that want to tear the psalmist apart are persecuting the psalmist. The petition for God to judge the psalmist and bring the evil to an end comes in verses 8–9:

The LORD judges the peoples;
   judge me, O LORD, according to my righteousness
   and according to the integrity that is in me.
O let the evil of the wicked come to an end,
   but establish the righteous,
you who test the minds and hearts,
   O righteous God."

9. Remember (1994, 110–11)

The petition for God to remember, says Miller, occurs primarily in communal lament psalms, as opposed to personal ones. Psalmists make three primary appeals for God to remember. One is that God not remember the sins of the faithful ones who are praying for help. The second appeal is for God to remember the words and deeds of the psalmist's enemies. The third appeal is for God to remember God's own ways, God's character, God's covenant with the people, and what the people have done to keep their covenant with God. An example is Psalm 79, in which Jerusalem and the temple have been destroyed, and the blood of executed Hebrews is flowing. Following a petition against the enemy in verses 6–7, in this case enemy nations, a petition for God to remember occurs in the first part of verse 8, followed by a petition for grace and mercy in the second part:

> Do not remember against us the iniquities of our
> ancestors;
> let your compassion come speedily to meet us,
> for we are brought very low.

10. Blessing (1994, 112)

The petition for God to bless the psalmist, or the community, is not typical in lament psalms. It appeals for God to look favorably upon the psalmist or for God to provide for the ongoing needs of life in the sense of providence, and it may be paired with a petition for help. Psalm 109 is an extraordinary example. The psalmist is treated horribly and needs deliverance desperately. In the midst of other kinds of petition comes the petition for blessing in verse 28:

> Let them curse, but you will bless.
> Let my assailants be put to shame; may your
> servant be glad.

11. Instruction and Guidance (1994, 112–14)

The final kind of petition is the petition for divine instruction and guidance. According to Miller, this petition is "a plea for an *ongoing* work of God, a continuing direction for life, instilling in the petitioner an understanding of God's will and God's way." As a petition in a lament psalm, it is in the context of a prayer for help against enemies. "The psalmist knows that the Lord's way is in some sense a way out of the predicament. Persistence in the way of righteousness will bring a vindication against the unrighteous enemy" (112–13).

An example is Psalm 5:8:

> Lead me, O LORD, in your righteousness
> because of my enemies;
> make your way straight before me.

Petitions of Contemporary Psalmists of Lament

Contemporary psalms of lament include the petition, appealing to God for intervention and deliverance. The appeal to God for help has content informed by the fourth mourning process, relinquishing attachments to the deceased and the contemporary psalmist's old assumptive world. Numerous possible contemporary petitions can relate to relinquishing attachments. I will discuss a few in this section, but others are just as viable.

Petitions for Help with Resistance to Relinquishing Attachments

Recently, I saw a television show in which one of the main characters had a resistance to relinquishing a particular attachment to his deceased wife. The show was a British murder mystery featuring a team of police officers. As the show begins, one of the detectives, accompanied by a colleague, is sitting in a lawyer's office hesitating to sign a document despite encouragement and reassurances from the lawyer, a trustworthy friend. Finally, he walks out without signing it. Not until the end of the show do viewers find out what the opening scene was about, as he explains to his colleague why he resisted signing the document: The document is his will, and he needs to remove his wife's name from it because she is dead. But he has been unable to force himself to sign the updated will.

The will represents a significant tie to the detective's wife, and he is resisting letting go of it, or relinquishing this attachment. As Rando noted above, the mourner may not want to give up a particular tie to the deceased for a variety of personal reasons, many of which involve fear and change. Another kind of reason may involve pressures to relinquish the tie before the mourner is ready. The pressure may come from another person or from practical circumstances. In the case of the detective, some pressure to relinquish a particular tie is due to a practical circumstance, updating his will. I will discuss personal reasons for such resistance in the next section.

In the face of resistance to relinquishing a particular attachment, one possible kind of petition is a petition for grace and mercy, like Psalm 31:9:

> Be gracious to me, O Lord, for I am in distress;
> my eye wastes away from grief,
> my soul and body also.

The contemporary petition for grace and mercy could be:

> *Give me your grace and compassion, O Lord, for I am in*
> *   pain;*
> *the tension of living with the need to sign the will fills me*
> *   with distress.*

Petitions for Help with Relinquishing Attachments to the Deceased

The detective explained to his colleague why he resisted signing the revised will. His wife's signature had been on several documents jointly with his signature, including the mortgage, auto loans, and bank accounts, as well as the will. Every one of these jointly signed documents represented ways in which they shared life together, and all of them had to be revised, with her signature removed from them. The will was the last one left to change. Revising it was too overwhelming, so he had put off signing it.

The jointly signed documents symbolize powerful attachments. One kind, for example, is shared ownership of property. A house, for instance, may just be a building made of wood or brick, but it also is the home where a marriage evolves. It may be where children are raised, where growth in the relationship occurs over time, where special family gatherings are held for years. Another kind of attachment is financial, symbolized by joint bank accounts, as the partners develop ways of managing their financial affairs. This reflects how they work out decision making for spending and saving. The third kind of jointly signed document, the will, also relates to property and money, but puts them in a more profound context, the end of the relationship due to death. Both partners know that each will die at some point with one going first, but that point is out there in the future. How hard it must be to deal with a will when one partner dies, because it forces the mourner to confront the end of the relationship, as well as the death of the loved one.

Signing the revised will caused the detective to face the end of his marriage and the death of his wife yet again. Now, he told his colleague, he was ready to sign it. In a situation like this, a contemporary psalmist of lament may offer a petition seeking God's attention, like Psalm 17:1:

> Hear a just cause, O LORD; attend to my cry;
> give ear to my prayer from lips free of deceit.

The mourner does not expect God to make the situation magically different. It can be encouraging to know God is aware of the mourner's situation and takes it seriously, strengthening the mourner for relinquishing a particular attachment. The petition of the detective, for example, could be:

> *Hear me, O Lord, for I must face my loss once more;*
> *Attend to my anxiety about signing the will;*
> *Listen to my request, and be with me as I move ahead.*

Petitions for Help with Old Specific Assumptions

The detective could not help but focus on the common thread, the removal of his wife's signature, running through the documents needing to be changed following his wife's death. It was as if physical evidence of their life together was being destroyed one document at a time. Signing new documents, minus his wife's signature, meant letting go of particular connections to his dead wife, but it also meant having to deal with the part of his assumptive world specifically involving his relationship with his wife.

The old documents, those in force while his wife was still alive, conveyed something about his status as a married person. For example, consider the will. Perhaps, for the entire marriage he had assumed that his wife would outlive him, because he was older than she and because of the potential of him being killed in his line of work. A corresponding assumption would be that his status as a married person never would change. Now, however, following her death, he no longer has the same status. Instead, society has bestowed upon him a new status as a widower, which affects his identity, his legal standing, and how others in society will view him and relate to him. His old assumptions, that his wife would outlive him and that he always would have the same status, must be relinquished. Signing a new will not only involves relinquishing an attachment to his dead wife, but also involves giving up related assumptions about her life and his status.

Relinquishing an old assumption goes hand-in-hand with developing a new one, or at least revising an old one. This means the assumptive lens through which oneself, relationships, and the world have been seen is changing. The lens will be different, and the perception of reality will be different to the degree that the assumptive world changes. This can sound rather scary. Who knows exactly what new specific assumptions should be? They certainly cannot be known ahead of time so as to prevent having to take a risk.

In this time of transition, one possible petition may be the petition for protection. In Psalm 25, the psalmist expresses concern about being shamed in verse 1. Then, in verse 20, the petitioner asks for divine protection:

O guard my life, and deliver me;
  do not let me be put to shame, for I take refuge in
  you.

The detective's petition for protection may be something like this:

Guard my life, God, as I abandon assumptions
I have held for many years about my status and my wife.
Be my refuge as I go through a scary transition
into new ways of seeing myself, my relationships, and the world.

Petitions for Help with Old Global Assumptions

As an experienced member of the police force, the detective surely has seen more than his share of human tragedy, family dysfunction, and death. Yet when death struck his own family, his global assumptions, such as assumptions about human nature, relationships, and God were subject to questioning and change in ways he may not have expected, even with his professional experience.

Imagine, for example, that his marriage helped him maintain a positive view of life in the face of the evil he witnessed in his work. This could be associated with one of the fundamental assumptions discussed above, that the world is benevolent. Now, his wife is gone, and he cannot help but entertain a more negative, perhaps even cynical, view that he had managed to keep at bay previously. He is beginning to feel less safe.

One possible petition is a petition for instruction and guidance like Psalm 5:8:

Lead me, O LORD, in your righteousness
   because of my enemies;
   make your way straight before me.

The detective as a contemporary psalmist of lament senses that growing into a balanced and positive view of the world, and avoiding cynicism, can only come by learning more of teachings about God and following God's ways. His petition could be:

Lead me, Lord, in just ways,
in the face of an evil and unfair world.
Show me the way ahead,
and grant me greater wisdom about life.

This is not a petition for keeping his assumption about the benevolence of the world exactly the same as it was before his wife's death. Rather, it seeks God's help for growing into a more profound and meaningful outlook on the world in which he lives and works.

Implications for the Ministry of Lament

What could be more familiar to congregations than petitioning God for intervention and deliverance? Individuals pray for help. People pray together for help in small groups and classes. The congregation prays for help in worship. The appeals range far and wide, from wanting healing to requesting that war end. Regarding grief, if this chapter conveys anything, it is that the possible petitions to God for help in situations of bereavement also range far and wide. Even when a single attachment must be relinquished, the possibilities for petitions are multiple.

In the ministry of lament, pastors and congregations realize that grieving people wrestle with relinquishing attachments to the deceased and to the old assumptive world. They also recognize the different kinds of attachments, some associated with practical matters and others profoundly global and theological. The congregation and its leaders affirm that some attachments need to be relinquished, though pastors and church members do not pressure a mourner to give up a tie to the deceased or an old assumption. Finally, the church affirms that grief and mourning do not require giving up all ties to the deceased.

While petitions in the lament psalms are suggestive for contemporary petitions of mourners, they also provide possibilities for practicing the ministry of lament with mourners who are wrestling with relinquishing attachments. One possibility involves changing the overall attitude of the congregation in their communal life. For example, just as the psalmist asks God for grace and mercy, so the congregation can work on developing a greater atmosphere of compassion for and acceptance of those who mourn and must relinquish attachments. Another possibility comes from the petition for instruction and guidance. Just as the psalmist recognizes that help requires learning and following God's will and ways, as Miller stated above, so those who learn together in small groups and classes should know that their study can impact the fourth mourning process, relinquishing attachments, as much as any other area of life. A third possibility involves worship. Petitions in the lament psalms can be related to the fourth mourning process in sermons, and petitions in prayers can be greatly expanded to include various aspects of this part of mourning. Virtually all of the petitions in the lament psalms can inform the ministry of lament, and a class exploring the possibilities can be one way of developing the ministry of lament in a congregation.

Finally, in private pastoral care conversation, and in a small group setting, the petition provides the opportunity for a pastor or church member to ask a bereaved conversation partner a simple question: "What kind of help would you like to request from God?" This question, or one similar to it, can precede an actual prayer incorporating the answer to the question. Or it can lead to discussion about God's help and what the mourner needs in terms of relinquishing old attachments.

Conclusion

In this chapter, the focus has been on rewriting a bereaved life story as it involves relinquishing attachments, the fourth mourning process. The part of the story involving the mourner's relationship with God focuses on the petition in the lament psalms. As a psalmist of lament, the mourner seeks God's help for relinquishing particular ties to the deceased and the old assumptive world. In the ministry of lament, petition provides guidance in caring for bereaved people who are wrestling with relinquishing attachments.

CHAPTER 7

Confidence in God

Because the ministry of lament is a long-term caring ministry, those who practice it can expect to see positive changes associated with the later mourning processes. Now, it is time to discuss the third and final phase of grief, because the last two mourning processes relate to it. The fifth, and next to last, mourning process addresses several important features of a bereaved life story at this juncture, and the fifth part of the lament psalms shows the next aspect of the mourner's relationship with God. The focus on contemporary psalmists of lament shifts increasingly to life taking shape in the present, as the bereaved life story continues being rewritten. The chapter concludes with implications for the ministry of lament.

The Final Phase of Grief

Rando names the third phase of grief the accommodation phase. In this phase, the most intensely painful part of grief is giving way to an increasing emphasis on reestablishing life gradually in the everyday world without the lost loved one. Accommodation means that the grieving person is making room for the loss in present life, in the recognition that a relationship will always survive with the deceased person, psychologically speaking, and that the future will contain upsurges of grief. Rando describes the main feature of the third phase this way: "The deceased is not forgotten, nor is the loss; however, the mourner learns to live with cognizance of the death and its implications in a way that does not preclude healthy, life-affirming growth" (1993, 40).

By using the term accommodation to describe this phase, Rando seeks to avoid conveying that there is, or should be, a final, complete ending to grief. It is rather like what Dennis Klass describes as "resolved as much as it will be," when he characterizes the final part of grief among parents who have lost a child (2001, 80).

Accommodating the loss reminds me of an elderly church member I once visited. As we talked, she told me that her middle-aged son had died four years earlier due to a tragic accident, and she showed me his picture. Following my condolences, she went on to say that she no longer grieved his loss. At the time, I wondered about her statement. As I got to know her better, I understood that her unending love for her son went hand-in-hand with the "life-affirming growth" characterizing her life in the present. I believe that she was making room for her loss in daily life and that she was able to live in a healthy manner, not that she never had upsurges of grief.

I might have found a different situation. She could have been stuck in an early part of her grief for years, having avoided many of the mourning processes. Her relationship with God could have remained fixed on the complaint, in which she blamed God perpetually for her loss. In this case, she never would have been able to write the next part of her contemporary psalm of lament, confessing the trust that could have opened up the possibility of petitioning God for help with her deep sorrow. Instead, she avoided this negative scenario and was learning to live in the present fruitfully. The things involved in learning to live in the present, accommodating the loss, are the sorts of things addressed in the fifth mourning process.

The Fifth Mourning Process:
Readjust to Move Adaptively into the New World
without Forgetting the Old

If you own and drive a car, you normally adjust its various features to fit you. The driver's seat is moved closer or farther away from the steering wheel depending on your size and preference. You adjust the rearview mirror and the outside mirrors so you can see traffic. You preset the radio so your favorite station is easily accessible. You set the air conditioning the way you want it. Adjusting something means that you alter it, move it, or adapt it to fit your situation so you can function appropriately. If another person drives your car, that person may readjust some features of the car, such as the rearview mirror. Readjusting is simply adjusting again to fit a different situation.

When Rando names the fifth mourning process in terms of readjusting (readjust to move adaptively into the new world without forgetting the old) she is saying that the mourner is adjusting again, adapting to the new world, the world as it exists now for the mourner after the loved one has died. Some readjustments may be practical and unavoidable, such as the need to establish a procedure and routine for paying bills. Other readjustments may be philosophical. For example, a global assumption about humanity or the world may have been shattered and must be addressed.

A mourner moves adaptively into the new world without forgetting the old. As the accommodation phase of grief makes clear, readjusting must happen in a way that makes room for the loss in the present. According to Rando, "In this 'R' process, the individual takes steps to accommodate the loss." This includes retaining some attachments from before the death: "Contrary to prevailing myth, it is clear that... she can retain certain connections with the old world that need not compromise healthy adjustment in the new one" (1993, 52).

In many ways, this mourning process completes what was begun in the last one. According to Rando, "Accommodation transpires in the internal realm, with revised assumptions about the world, an altered relationship with the deceased, and the formation of a new identity. It also takes place in the external realm, with adaptations in behavior." The old assumptive world is giving way to revision. The mourner has relinquished particular old attachments, but is developing a new relationship with the deceased. An old part of the mourner's identity is gone, but a new one is being formed. Some old behaviors cannot be sustained, but now adaptations in behavior are being made (1993, 52).

Finally, Rando points out that these four areas needing readjustment are interrelated and influence one another. A change in the assumptive world, for instance, may lead to a consequent change in behavior (1993, 429).

Relating Anew to the Deceased

If readjusting to move adaptively into the new world includes not forgetting the old, one mainstay of not forgetting is an ongoing relationship with the deceased. Rando speaks to this quite pointedly:

> Mourners and caregivers must recognize that it is not unnatural, pathological, or indicative of inability to deal with reality if an individual does not want to sever all connection to one she [or he] has held dear…Human beings are symbolic creatures. We do not need a concrete presence to have a relationship. As such, it is not uncommon, nor does it disregard reality, to want to keep a special place in one's life for a special person and to want at times to interact symbolically with that loved one. The question should not be, Is wanting to maintain a connection with a deceased loved one wrong? but rather, What is an appropriate connection and what conditions promote it? (1993, 54)

According to Rando, the appropriateness of this relationship can be judged under two criteria. The first relates to something discussed in chapter 3. Recall Joan Didion's year of magical thinking in which she found herself repeatedly expecting her deceased husband to return. Getting past the magical thinking is the first criterion: "the mourner must truly recognize that the loved one is dead and fully understand the implications of this." The second criterion relates to the mourning process being discussed in this chapter: "the mourner must continue to move forward adaptively into the new life" (Rando, 1993, 436).

Rando discusses several ways that mourners engage in an appropriate relationship with a deceased loved one. The first way involves developing an image of the deceased person with which the mourner will interact. This relates to the third mourning process discussed in chapter five, involving remembering the deceased realistically. "The good and bad, the happy and sad, the fulfilling and the unfulfilling—all aspects of the person, relationship, and experience must be reviewed, felt, and integrated. Based on all of this, the mourner develops a composite image of the loved one" (1993, 56).

The second way of relating to the deceased is dynamic, as opposed to fixed or static. For instance, as the mourner ages, new insights may emerge about the deceased. If a child loses a parent, for example, when the child becomes an adult, the adult child should not continue relating to the deceased parent as if the adult child were still in grade school. (Rando, 1993, 50).

The third way involves decision making, involving what to retain from the old life and what to abandon. For instance, Rando uses the example of someone choosing to keep a routine of taking a walk on Sunday morning, a walk formerly taken with the deceased. This could be positive for the mourner. However, the mourner also should feel free to discontinue the walks if so desired (1993, 56).

The fourth way involves sensing the presence of the deceased. This includes everything from hallucinatory experiences to a sense of the deceased's presence, and communication in the form of reviewing important events, asking for guidance about a problem, or prayer. Actively recalling memories, connection with the deceased (e.g., a special song or certain location), and dreaming are other ways in which mourners maintain and nourish their relationship with the lost loved ones. (Rando, 1993, 57)

The fifth way involves what psychotherapists call identification. This may involve such things as taking on values of the deceased, for example, and altering one's personality to internalize this change (Rando, 1993, 57).

The sixth way is through ritual. This may include such things as anniversary celebrations and doing something in the name of the lost loved one. It does not need to be dramatic, but may be as simple as perusing the family photograph album (Rando, 1993, 58).

The seventh way is through focusing on tangible objects. This may include anything from jewelry, to creations of the deceased such as paintings, to symbolic reminders of the deceased such as a shared home (Rando, 1993, 58).

The eighth way involves the life of the mourner in the present as it has to do with keeping the memory of the deceased alive. This may include such things as carrying on a family tradition, considering the beliefs and perspectives of the deceased when actions must be taken, and so forth (Rando, 1993, 58).

Revising the Assumptive World

As we saw in the last chapter, the assumptive world involves the entire network of specific and global assumptions through which the mourner perceives and interprets reality. Readjustments to it must be appropriate for life in the present, and they must allow for accommodation of the loss (Rando, 1993, 430).

Readjusting the assumptive world involves many different possible scenarios in which revised and new assumptions must become integrated into the entire network. Some assumptions may be shattered quickly—such as after a sudden, tragic death—and demand immediate attention. Other assumptive changes may happen more gradually and subtly as life following the death evolves. Some readjustments may relate to assumptions associated with the death directly, while others may relate to secondary losses arising as a result of the death, such as the loss of a home (Rando, 1993, 52–53).

New Ways of Being in the World

Readjusting behavior, says Rando, involves becoming accustomed to the world as it is now, with the deceased no longer present physically. For example, needs formerly met by the deceased now must be fulfilled in other ways. Rando gives the example of a person having the habit of talking to her sister about her stress. Now, since her sister is dead, she must find another way to address her stress. Adapting to the present world may require such things as learning new skills, discovering new roles, or making new friends (1993, 58–59).

A New Identity

Recall the detective in the previous chapter. His status changed from being a married person to being a widower. This necessarily affected his image of himself, because his identity had included being married. Now his identity had to change to reflect his new status. Add to this revising other parts of his assumptive world, readjusting his behaviors, and developing new ways of relating to his deceased wife, and clearly his identity cannot remain as it was before his wife's death. Now, his answer to the question, "Who am I?" must be readjusted to reflect the many changes he is experiencing. According to Rando, "Over time, the mourner must develop a perspective on what has been lost or gained in the self. That which has been changed...must be recognized and mourned; that which continues must be affirmed; that which is new must be incorporated. The mourner will then need to integrate the new and old selves" (1993, 445).

The Fifth Part of the Lament Psalms: Words of Assurance

If the confession of trust preceding the petition expresses confidence in God in spite of the difficulty found in the complaint, the part of the psalm following the petition expresses certainty that the prayer for help will be heard and the petition answered. Anderson names this expression of certainty "words of assurance" (2000, 61).

An example comes from Psalm 28. In verses 3–4, the psalmist petitions God, requesting that enemies be repaid according to their deeds. Then, in verse 5, the psalmist expresses certainty, or assurance, that God will respond:

> Because they do not regard the works of the LORD,
>   or the work of his hands,
>   he will break them down and build them up no
>   more.

Notice that the psalmist is expressing certainty about something God will do at some point in the future. At this level, the words of assurance are another manifestation of the confession of trust. However, instead of being an expression of confidence in God's reliability in spite of the complaint, it is an expression of certainty, a firm trust, that God will hear the petition and will respond. Nonetheless, if the words of assurance were nothing more than part of the confession of trust, the words of assurance would not be identified as a different part of the lament psalms. There must be more to the story.

The Oracle of Salvation

Anderson introduces another feature of the words of assurance that makes all the difference. Contemporary scholars refer to this feature as the oracle of salvation. Imagine that you are participating in the ancient worship of Israel and a lament psalm is part of the liturgy. The congregation recites the psalm together, through the petition. Then, the priest speaks the next part of the psalm to the congregation. This part of the psalm that the priest speaks is the oracle of salvation. It is words that "assured the suppliant of God's grace and favor." These words of assurance represent the words of God assuring the people, not just expressions of trust by the people toward God. In other words, it is a way of talking about how God responds as a conversation partner in the prayer, or how God answers prayer. After hearing these words of assurance, the congregation concludes the psalm with thanksgiving and praise in response to the assurance they have received. There is a problem, however. None of the oracles of salvation in the psalms has been preserved. The best that can be said about them is that some psalms contain hints that they once were spoken in the liturgy, with Psalm 85 providing an important example (Anderson, 2000, 99).

Miller points to Psalm 85:8 as an oracle that the liturgical leader could have spoken, introducing the oracle of salvation:

> Let me hear what God the Lord will speak,
> for he will speak peace to his people,
> to his faithful, to those who turn to him in their hearts.

In this instance, the divine word of assurance will be one of peace (1994, 140).

Anderson suggests that verses 9–10 summarize what would have been the actual oracle of salvation (2000, 99):

> Surely his salvation is at hand for those who fear him,
> that his glory may dwell in our land.
> Steadfast love and faithfulness will meet;
> righteousness and peace will kiss each other.

One significant reason biblical scholars can associate the psalms with the oracle of salvation is that it is found elsewhere in the scriptures in more complete form. Miller says Isaiah 40–55 (Second Isaiah) is especially valuable in this regard (1994, 142). The Israelites are exiled from their homeland and hope that God will deliver them. The oracle of salvation is presented in familiar prophetic terms, as the speech of God. In Isaiah 41:8–13, God says:

But you, Israel, my servant,
    Jacob, whom I have chosen,
    the offspring of Abraham, my friend;
you whom I took from the ends of the earth,
    and called from its farthest corners,
saying to you, "You are my servant,
    I have chosen you and not cast you off";
do not fear, for I am with you,
    do not be afraid, for I am your God;
I will strengthen you, I will help you,
    I will uphold you with my victorious right hand.
Yes, all who are incensed against you
    shall be ashamed and disgraced;
those who strive against you
    shall be as nothing and shall perish.
You shall seek those who contend with you,
    but you shall not find them;
those who war against you
    shall be as nothing at all.
For I, the LORD your God,
    hold your right hand;
it is I who say to you, "Do not fear,
    I will help you."

This passage, Miller points out, contains the main features of many oracles of salvation, though not all. First, it is a direct address to the one or group who prays, or it is specific as opposed to being a generalized address. Second, it contains an allusion to the plight or lament of the ones praying. Third, the heart of the oracle of salvation is the message of God, do not fear. It may be expressed poetically in different ways, such as encouragement not to be dismayed or discouraged. Fourth, the reason, or basis, for not being afraid is given, and it has two parts. The first part is the assurance that God is with the person or group. The second part is that God intends to help or deliver the petitioners from their trouble. Fifth, the oracle of salvation may elaborate the ways that God is going to help, presented in the future tense (1994, 142–47).

In addition to the prophets, writes Miller, many biblical narratives show not only what God promises, but also specifically how God helps. For instance, children are born to barren parents, water is found in the desert in the nick of time, and the sick are healed. The psalms, however, lack a narrative context informing readers about the specifics of God's response to the psalmist. Instead, the psalmist gives allusions to God answering the prayer for help in the lament psalms. This means that God's words of assurance to the petitioner, alluded to in the part of the psalm that points toward a full-fledged oracle of salvation, has to do with God answering the psalmist's prayer for help (1994, 170–71).

Among several examples, Miller points toward Psalm 12. In this psalm, God speaks words of assurance in the first person. The distraught psalmist appeals to God, and God responds in verse 5:

> "Because the poor are despoiled, because the needy groan,
> I will now rise up," says the LORD;
> "I will place them in the safety for which they long."

An Important Variation on a Theme

Finally, Miller discusses a variation on the theme of the words of assurance, a variation that has significance for contemporary psalmists of lament and the ministry of lament. Some lament psalms have no oracle of salvation in which God speaks words of assurance in the sense I have discussed. Instead, the psalmist, having made the petition, writes what would be the equivalent of a confession of trust if the words were about what God will do in the future. Sometimes the psalmist does something different. Instead of focusing on the future, the psalmist writes about the present, indicating that God already has responded to the prayer. Consequently, right then and there, the mood of the psalmist changes "from sorrow and complaint to joy, praise, and thanksgiving" (1994, 173).

Psalm 6 is a good example. The psalmist seeks divine help during a difficult time of languishing, experiencing terror, moaning in pain, and crying in bed at night. This troubled person petitions God for deliverance from the horrible nightmare of a situation. Then, following the petition, the psalmist expresses words of assurance in verses 8–9:

> Depart from me, all you workers of evil,
>   for the LORD has heard the sound of my weeping.
> The LORD has heard my supplication;
>   the LORD accepts my prayer.

The psalmist has been heard, and the words of assurance express this as a present reality, not something expected in the future. This raises questions fundamental to the nature of prayer and fundamental for understanding this part of the lament psalms. How does the psalmist know that the Lord has heard the supplication, that is, the petition? How is the psalmist able to make the assertion that the Lord accepts the psalmist's prayer? Miller's answer indicates that the psalmist is not merely reciting a formulaic response. Instead, the psalmist is expressing what is the case based on the experience of God having responded to the prayer: "The claim that God has heard the prayer...is so sure and the reversal of the psalm so sharp that one can account for all of that only on the premise that a word of assurance and salvation has been received from the Lord, an oracle of salvation" (1994, 173).

Words of Assurance of Contemporary Psalmists of Lament

A contemporary psalm of lament contains words of assurance. The fifth mourning process, readjusting to move adaptively into the new world without forgetting the old, provides the content informing this part of the psalm. Because this is a pretty massive mourning process, it will be helpful to focus on the four areas of readjustment discussed by Rando, including readjusting the assumptive world, identity, relating to the deceased, and behavior. One contemporary psalmist of lament may need to focus on one of these areas more than the others. Another may focus on several, seen as influencing each other. Or different areas may come into focus at different times.

Because this part of the lament psalm involves God responding, it is not something that can be the same for everyone by any means. In some instances, the contemporary words of assurance may need to be an expression of certainty that God will hear the prayer. In other instances, the contemporary psalmist may have the experience of God responding already, and the words of assurance will be more akin to the oracle of salvation. As Miller says above, God's message, do not be afraid, involves both assurance of God's abiding presence with the psalmist and assurance of help.

An excellent example of a contemporary psalmist's words of assurance appears in *Reflections on Grief and Spiritual Growth* (2005), edited by Andrew J. Weaver and Howard W. Stone. Duane Bidwell's chapter, "We Will Be Changed: Resurrection and Grief," recalls his experience of mourning the loss of someone he knew when he was a chaplain. His story culminates in what I believe can be interpreted as his words of assurance.

One Pastoral Theologian's Words of Assurance

Bidwell writes about the death of a client, Kent, a gay man, whom he came to know when he was executive director of an HIV/AIDS ministry. They developed a friendship lasting for several years until Kent's death. Though Kent was seriously ill, the illness did not kill him. Instead, he was murdered. In the beginning of the chapter, Bidwell tells about two important parts of his assumptive world, his attitude toward heaven and resurrection and his understanding of grief, both seen in relation to his work as a professional caregiver:

> I would nod and smile—benignly, I hope—when a grieving husband or distraught lover started talking about heaven. It's a little embarrassing to admit, but there it is: while the man or woman or child in front of me talked about streets of gold or a new body free

of pain or a joyful heavenly reunion in some timeless future or eternity with God, I would think, "Wow, cool, groovy; how nice that you've found a metaphor that works for you." (2005, 40)

Bidwell goes on to say that for most of his life, heaven and resurrection were, for him, "metaphors, constructs, temporary ways of making sense of death" that would be swept away in the storm of grief, finally to be replaced by something else to which the grieving person would cling. Then, life could continue. He identifies the view of grief undergirding his understanding of heaven and resurrection as a version of the twentieth-century view of grief similar to the view characterized by letting go and moving on, discussed in chapter two. Kent's death changed all this (2005, 40).

Bidwell begins his recollection and reexperiencing of Kent by describing him as HIV positive and as a massage therapist. In contrast, he describes himself as "a nerdy intellectual, married to a woman." Acknowledging that on the surface they were unlikely friends, Bidwell expresses how important Kent's presence was for him. He writes much of his chapter in a newly opened gallery and coffee bar across the street from Kent's favorite bar, writing to Kent as if writing a letter. His description of the people and the scene at this familiar location leads to an expression of loss:

There's no place else in this city where I'm surrounded by so many people who knew you; and when I see them and think how much you would love this place and then remember you're gone, a fresh awareness of loss slices through my chest—not grief, exactly, or sadness, but an awareness that my life is supposed to include you and you're not here. (2005, 41–42)

Then, Bidwell shifts into a different vein of writing, rather like the sudden shifts between the different parts of the lament psalms. He recalls how Kent was murdered and launches into what can only be called a complaint. He complains about an enemy, which in this instance is the dominant culture: "Kent's death was, for me, a textbook example of *disenfranchised grief*—loss not recognized or validated by the dominant culture." One part of this disenfranchisement involved friendship and the lack of words in the English language to characterize the richness of such a relationship: "I was continually frustrated by my inability to offer a relational term that succinctly explained to others why his death was so significant for me or that signaled the profundity of my loss. North American culture fails, for the most part, to recognize the depth of grief that can be associated with the loss of a friend" (2005, 42).

The second part of this disenfranchisement involved such things as Kent's sexual orientation, the manner of his death, and the circumstances surrounding it. Just as the dominant culture marginalized Kent, so Bidwell's relationship to Kent also was marginalized, resulting in lack of support in places he most needed it:

> In fact, the places where I most needed support when he died—at my work and church communities—were the places where others seemed most confused by, and uncomfortable with, the depth of my grief and the circumstances of Kent's death...only with my spouse and closest friends, and the AIDS community, did my loss feel real and valid. As a result, I began to draw false boundaries around my grief, discounting it to others and to myself. (2005, 42)

Next, Bidwell recalls some meaningful, yet painful, aspects of his relationship with Kent, who was not expected to live for more than five years, though he lived for eight. Death was an ongoing factor in their relationship, which brought about grief in anticipation of Kent's death and intimacy in their relationship: "I find it impossible to articulate the intimacy that comes when death brings two people together and they commit not to ignore this invisible third partner in their relationship." He recalls ways that he prepared for delivering Kent's eulogy and ways that he cared for Kent during hospitalizations (2005, 43).

Then, a surprise happened. Kent began improving dramatically and fell in love with a man named Blaise, with whom he bought a house and set up a domestic routine. This part of remembering is positive, but it quickly turns sad. A former lover of Blaise stalked them, causing all sorts of trouble, but the police never intervened. Finally, an intruder ends up killing Kent as he chased the intruder down the block.

This leads to the recollection of conversations between Bidwell and Kent about life after death, most often happening during massages. He says Kent believed in life after death and was curious about what was on the other side. "He would only say that he was certain life did not end, that his energy—and our shared energy—would continue." Bidwell recalls that during these times he would feel "the current of *élan vital*" course between them, and he would respond, "I hope you're right. I hope you're right." Perhaps these words, "I hope you're right," are Bidwell's wistful petition, a kind of hope against hope, or a longing, for life to continue in some sense (2005, 44).

Days after the funeral, late one night, Bidwell is sitting at his desk, on which resides an icon of Christ. He is reading Mark 8, in which Jesus touches a blind man's eyes and heals his blindness. The reference to touch reminds him of Kent, bringing on tears of grief. Then something totally unexpected happens, resulting in profound changes in his assumptive world, his identity as a Christian, his relationship to Kent, and his professional behavior.

As he sits there grieving, Bidwell feels a gentle energy on his shoulder. He raises his head, and his eyes lock with the eyes of Christ peering at him from the icon. He feels the energy binding them together and has a sudden realization. His description of this realization surely becomes his implicit words of assurance, for he has been assured:

> In an instant, I knew wholly that the healing touch I had experienced with Kent for so many years had been Christ's touch all along. It had not disappeared with Kent; it was present in all things...What

happened was simply this: my eyes were opened, and I recognized Christ—and Kent—in a new way (2005, 45).

Bidwell explains that the experience was not overly dramatic, but was ordinary and unreal simultaneously. He asks the same sorts of questions as Buechner asked earlier in chapter five: "Would it be accurate to say I encountered Kent's energy, alive in death?" His answer to such questions also is similar to Buechner's: "I cannot answer them." Yet he goes on to articulate the profound changes in his assumptive world that have occurred due to this experience, including his view of life beyond death, his understanding of grief, and his understanding of relating to the deceased in the present. "Life beyond death is real, and in grief it is no longer necessary or desirable to break my attachments. Rather, authentic Christian grieving requires me to maintain a bond with the deceased, a connection that does not belong to us at all but comes from another source altogether…That bond is real!" (2005, 45).

Clearly, changes in his assumptive world are interrelated with the development of his relationship to Kent in the present, his identity as a Christian, and his professional behavior toward other mourners. He reports that he no longer smiles benignly "when a grieving person talks about heaven or resurrection." Instead, he addresses this issue with "respect and curiosity." Finally, he no longer views this subject as a tool of pastoral care, but instead sees it as a "Christian responsibility." In the ministry of lament, Bidwell is on target (2005, 46).

Seen as a contemporary psalmist of lament, Bidwell is articulating the variation on a theme of the words of assurance discussed above, that the psalmist has experienced God already having answered the prayer. Put in terms of the lament psalm, Bidwell's words of assurance could be something like this:

I knew that something was not right, Lord.
But you have responded to my longing for Kent.

You have made things right, a total surprise.
You have turned my sorrow into rejoicing,
because I have Kent, and I have you!
I live in your world from this time forward.

Implications for the Ministry of Lament

One evening at a fellowship dinner, I asked a group of women if they ever talked to their dead husbands. I was fairly young and inexperienced in such things, but I had read something about it and was curious. I was aware of grief stages, but the stages said nothing about this. The answers of these women surprised me. In a matter-of-fact, casual manner, they all affirmed that they talked to their dead loved ones quite often.

A year or so later, I visited a woman in her eighties who was a longtime church member. She had fallen and broken a bone and was homebound during recovery. As we talked, she told me about her husband who had been dead for twenty years. The thing I remember most is her letting me know that she told her dead husband good night every evening at bedtime, and this often accompanied a prayer. She then asked me if I thought doing that was all right. Fortunately, I remembered what the women had said at the fellowship dinner, and I was able to respond appropriately, saying that it seemed fine to me if she told her husband good night.

In the ministry of lament, pastors and the congregation affirm that mourners can have an appropriate relationship with the deceased in the new world. Whether or not individual caregivers can bear witness to this based on personal experience, they can have the knowledge that mourning includes developing an appropriate relationship to the deceased in the present.

The ministry of lament also affirms and supports the other three areas discussed in the fifth mourning process. Mourners may be in the process of developing a new identity. They may be experimenting with new behaviors as they become accustomed to present life without the deceased. They may be wrestling with profound changes in their assumptive world.

Then, just when one part of this seems settled, another may emerge, because all these areas are interrelated.

In situations where a global assumption about God has been shattered and the mourner is struggling with developing a new global assumption about God, those in the ministry of lament can be especially helpful. The psalms show how many ways God is described in the scriptures. The shattering of some understanding of God presents an opportunity to expand the understanding of God. The contemporary words of assurance may be an expression of certainty that God will hear and respond to the mourner's petition for help with developing a new and more profound understanding of God.

Pastors and congregations can prepare for the ministry of lament by studying the huge variety of ways God is described in the scriptures. It is not just the occasional mourner who needs to develop a broader, more expansive, more flexible, and often less comfortable view of God, it is everyone.

Finally, in the ministry of lament mourners are affirmed in their experiences of God's words of assurance and changes that result. This may be a sense of trust that God will hear and respond, though they may have no internal sense of that yet. This may be an internal change, when anxiety, guilt, or despair gives way to relief and comfort due to sensing God's presence. This may be a new hope that some concrete change in the situation is going to happen, though it has not yet come. This may be a new sense of confidence or courage accompanying the mourner's own effort to effect some adaptation to the new world. This may be an interpretation of something helpful that happened, an interpretation that this was the work of God.

Conclusion

The fifth mourning process is a hopeful one. It places the reality of loss in the context of developing new possibilities for fruitful living. Contemporary psalmists of lament move beyond petition to words of assurance, and the ministry of lament supports the rewriting of this aspect of the bereaved life story.

CHAPTER 8

The Dawn of Praise

The five mourning processes presented in the previous chapters show that rewriting a bereaved life story covers quite a wide-ranging territory. The sixth mourning process presented in this chapter brings a mourner's rewriting to a positive and forward-looking conclusion by helping that person embrace healthy living in the present for the long term. Likewise, the final part of the lament psalms presented in this chapter is a joyful culmination of lament. Contemporary psalmists of lament have the opportunity to complete their new psalm on a high note with the joy of genuine thanks and praise. Finally, this has important implications for the ministry of lament presented in the final part of the chapter.

The Sixth Mourning Process: Reinvest

Rando calls the sixth mourning process reinvest. If mourners must move adaptively into the new world without forgetting the old, they need emotional energy empowering them to do such things as develop and sustain new relationships and learn new behaviors. Otherwise, the mourner may be going through the motions but have no staying power. According to Rando, "the emotional energy that had been directed toward the preservation and maintenance of the former relationship with the loved one must be redirected toward rewarding new investments in other people, objects, roles, hopes, beliefs, causes, ideals, goals, pursuits, and so forth." In the sixth mourning process, then, mourners are transferring emotional energy formerly invested in the deceased loved one to the present, and they are redirecting it in the service of healthy living (1993, 60).

Emotional Energy

Everyone can relate to the idea of having enough energy for daily living. Stress, anxiety, work, becoming new parents, and other challenges of contemporary life make the energy needed for living fruitfully a valuable commodity. Having energy for investing in present life means having the vitality, the vigor, to make commitments, follow through on them, maintain relationships, and engage in the many different areas of life Rando mentioned above, living in the new world in rewarding and long-lasting ways.

The emotional aspect of this energy is especially important. Recall from the third mourning process, recollecting and reexperiencing the deceased and the relationship, that Rando describes the power of feelings by comparing them to a psychological electromagnetic current providing the magnetism that binds people together. This explains one reason why engaging in the third mourning process is important. Remembering and reexperiencing loosens ties with the deceased, freeing up emotional energy formerly invested in the deceased, so that it can be redirected toward others for living in the present.

Rando strongly affirms that no one can replace the person who died, "no one and nothing can take that person's place." She also affirms that some of the emotional energy freed for the present is used for the mourner's new relationship with the deceased rather than being redirected toward others. However, the new relationship with the deceased cannot absorb all the energy, or none will be available for other people or activities. Rather, the mourner's relationship with the deceased is part of a larger whole, in which the mourner also reinvests in other relationships, activities, pursuits, and so on, representing a life fully invested in present living (1993, 60).

The Image of Reinvestment

Imagine that a beloved family member has died, and you are the recipient of a large sum of money from a life insurance policy. You take this money and invest in the stock market to generate income. As dictionaries indicate, *to invest* means to spend money on something for the purpose of generating some desired result, such as making a profit or starting a business. Many congregations have widows and widowers who live on a "fixed income" based on investments made possible by life insurance policies.

Dictionaries also indicate that investing does not have to be about money. A person or group can invest time, effort, or energy in an undertaking to achieve many different kinds of desired results. For instance, a professional sports team may invest in promising young players by having coaches work with them to develop their skills. This is an investment involving time, effort, and commitment, not just money. The purpose of this investment involves achieving the desired result of having a better team capable of winning the championship.

When Rando discusses reinvesting emotional energy in relationships and other areas of life, she includes the notion that the investment has the purpose of achieving some desired result. This is the nature of investment. The key to understanding this is to look at the former relationship between the mourner and the deceased. Investment in that relationship yielded certain desired results for the one who now mourns. The results could have been many things, such as the joy of giving and receiving love, the expectation of having companionship, having certain needs and desires fulfilled, and sharing hopes for the future. Now, however, the mourner cannot receive these desired results from the relationship.

Instead, if the mourner is to have a healthy life in the present, emotional energy that was invested in the relationship with the deceased must be reinvested in new relationships and activities capable of yielding the desired results. This is not a matter of being selfish. Nothing is wrong with wanting a dinner companion, for instance, when the alternative is isolation and loneliness.

This redirection of energy is not meant to imply a one to one correspondence between the original investment in the deceased and the reinvestment. In the case of marriage, for example, the widow or widower does not have to remarry. Some investments may be in people, while others may be in new activities, such as volunteer work or returning to school. Some investments may be in material things, such as an art collection. Still others may involve pursuing a dream or becoming an officer in an organization. The main point is that the mourner invests energy and receives an appropriate satisfaction in return (Rando, 1993, 60 and 449).

Blocks to Reinvesting

A husband cared for his sick wife for three years, until she died of cancer. Within a month following her death, he met someone new through the Internet. In six months, they were married. Four more months passed, and they were divorced. This husband thought he had grieved enough during his wife's long illness. He did not realize he still needed to grieve and mourn following the death. Consequently, the second marriage did not represent genuine reinvestment, but instead was a way of avoiding grief and mourning. At the very least, he needed time to experience living in the aftermath of his wife's death, before prematurely reinvesting in a new relationship and marriage. Now, he was forced to cope with a more complicated situation involving divorce as well as death.

Others who care for loved ones during a long-term illness have the opposite response. According to Rando, "After so much time devoted to caretaking, they often are so depleted and unused to living a life for themselves that they have difficulty readjusting." The type of death can make a difference in the ability of the mourner to engage in reinvesting (1993, 449).

In addition to death following long-term illness, Rando lists several other kinds of death making such a difference, including "suicide, murder, AIDS-related deaths, auto erotic asphyxiation, and other types of death that tend to disenfranchise the mourner." Recall chaplain Bidwell's complaint in the last chapter, in which he describes having discounted to himself and others his grief over his gay friend's murder. The kind of difference such deaths may make is that the mourner receives little support and may withdraw from the support actually offered (Rando, 1993, 449).

Rando lists several additional situations having the potential to make reinvesting complicated. One is that the mourner may be acting on the basis of misinformation. For example, the mourner may equate the length of time, along with the amount, of suffering with love for the deceased. In this case, reinvestment becomes interpreted to mean that the mourner no longer misses the deceased, or that the relationship has declined in importance. Another kind of misinformation is that enjoying life again is insulting to the memory of the deceased. Such falsehoods can block the freedom of the mourner to reinvest (1993, 449).

Another kind of situation having potential to block reinvestment involves fear. Rando says some mourners fear being hurt again by caring for another person who also could be lost. In addition, some mourners fear others will view them as not having mourned enough if they reinvest in a new relationship. A third fear involves the personality of the mourner, such as being extremely dependent, or anxious, or lacking needed social or communication skills for negotiating adequately in a world that seems unfamiliar following the death. A fourth fear involves fear of the unknown. Finally, a fifth fear is one associated with an issue discussed frequently in these chapters, the fear that reinvestment marks the end of relating to the lost loved one (1993, 449).

Beyond Mourning: STUGS

Rando does not linger over the joy or hope associated with the sixth mourning process, nor does she reflect on any transition between engaging in reinvesting and living past the time when it was an intentional and new part of a mourner's life. Perhaps this is appropriate, given the significant changes taking place in understanding these things. Gone is a preconceived time frame for completing grief and mourning, such as a year, as well as any notion that no grief and mourning should occur in the future. Indeed, as congregations know well, those who have lost loved ones may experience brief bouts of grief many years after the death. This is what Rando, in dialogue with other psychologists, calls a subsequent temporary upsurge of grief, or STUG. This is a brief period in which the person experiences a new round of grief for the lost loved one, though the death may have been long ago (Rando, 1993, 64).

Rando divides the situations and events that stimulate the person to experience grief into three categories. The first one is called cyclic precipitants. It involves cyclical events and times, including anniversaries, holidays, different seasons of the year, and rituals, particularly rituals that were part of everyday life, or family life, such as gathering for family picnics at a special time and place. The second one is called linear precipitants. It involves one-time situations and events, rather than cyclical occurrences. It may be age-related or a milestone for which the dead family member cannot be present, such as a graduation. It can involve some new experience or transition, such as moving to a new home or city. The third category is called stimulus-cued precipitants. It involves situations and events unrelated to the passing of time, unlike the other two. This includes encountering something that stimulates memories associated with the deceased, such as unexpectedly hearing "our song" (Rando, 1993, 66–77).

The Sixth Part of the Lament Psalms: The Vow of Praise and Thanksgiving

The psalmists of lament express an abundance of joy in the final part of the lament psalms, called the vow of praise and thanksgiving. The psalmist has cried out for God's help during a terrible situation, expressing complaints and confessions of trust, petitions and words of assurance. The vow of praise and thanksgiving is hard won, arising in the context of trust and assurance that God will act.

This joyful vow is a sincere promise or commitment being made in the concluding part of the psalm. Anderson writes that this vow involves calling on the name of God, testifying before the community what God has done, and expressing exclamations of praise (2000, 62). Psalm 7:17 is an example:

> I will give to the LORD the thanks due to his
> righteousness,
>   and sing praise to the name of the LORD, the Most
> High.

Because the vow involves giving God both praise and thanks, you might think that the two words *praise* and *thanks* are just different ways of saying the same thing. In the psalms, this is not quite true. Biblical scholars see them as two closely interrelated forms of praising God.

Vowing to Give Thanks

Thanksgiving presents quite an interesting issue. Giving thanks involves expressing gratitude, according to the dictionaries. In the book of Psalms, lament psalms include giving thanks to God in the final part of the psalm. But giving thanks to God also is found in another kind of psalm, called the song of thanksgiving. This type of psalm is entirely about giving thanks. Anderson discusses the relationship between these two types of psalms, showing the connection they have regarding thanks. Comparing the two is a helpful way to shed light on giving thanks in the final part of the lament psalms.

The Lament Psalms. The difference between the two really is quite simple. In the certainty that God hears the psalmist's prayer, the psalmist of lament gives thanks. While the psalmist may give thanks for having been heard, ultimately the psalmist is giving thanks based on the assurance that God's saving action will happen in the future. The thanksgiving is future oriented. As Anderson says, "in the certainty of being heard by God, the suppliant—whether the community or the individual—looks forward to God's deliverance from a situation of limitation or distress," and in anticipation of this divine action the psalmist of lament expresses thanks (2000, 98).

Consider Psalm 28. The psalmist cries out to be heard by God, seeking refuge from the unscrupulous behavior of wicked and evil enemies. Following the petition for help and words of assurance, the psalmist expresses the vow of praise and thanks in verses 6–9. Verse 7 contains an explicit word of thanks:

> The LORD is my strength and my shield;
>> in him my heart trusts;
> so I am helped, and my heart exults,
>> and with my song I give thanks to him.

Song of Thanksgiving. Giving thanks in the song of thanksgiving is not a different kind of thanks than that found in the lament psalms. Rather, it is an expansion of the thanks, so that it becomes the focus of the entire psalm with one main difference. Instead of thanking God based on assurance of future divine deliverance, the song of thanksgiving expresses gratitude for divine deliverance that has happened already. As Anderson puts it, "These songs are sung by people who, after a time of waiting…have experienced the goodness of God in the everyday world" (2000, 100). An example is Psalm 118. Like other songs of thanksgiving, this one begins, in verse 1, with a focus on giving thanks:

> O give thanks to the LORD, for he is good;
>> his steadfast love endures forever!

In verse 5, the psalmist begins telling the reason for giving thanks in general terms:

> Out of my distress I called on the LORD;
>> the LORD answered me and set me in a broad place.

After extolling readers to have confidence in the Lord, the psalmist tells more specifically about the distress being experienced and how the Lord helped, in verses 10–14:

> All nations surrounded me;
>> in the name of the LORD I cut them off!
> They surrounded me, surrounded me on every side;
>> in the name of the LORD I cut them off!
> They surrounded me like bees;
>> they blazed like a fire of thorns;
>> in the name of the LORD I cut them off!
> I was pushed hard, so that I was falling,
>> but the LORD helped me.
> The LORD is my strength and my might;
>> he has become my salvation.

After more thanks and praise, the psalmist concludes by repeating verse 1.

The Song of Thanksgiving in Lament Psalms. Many expressions of giving thanks in the lament psalms do not qualify as full-blown songs of thanksgiving. Yet some of them do focus on thanks and praise to the point that they are identified as songs of thanksgiving, though the thanks still is future oriented and on a smaller scale. Above, I quoted Psalm 28:7 as an example of thanks in lament psalms. Verses 6 and 7 together constitute a small song of thanksgiving:

> Blessed be the LORD,
>> for he has heard the sound of my pleadings.
> The LORD is my strength and my shield;
>> in him my heart trusts;
> so I am helped, and my heart exults,
>> and with my song I give thanks to him.

The main focus of the thanks is the certainty that God has heard the prayer, but the saving action of God still is in the future. This future orientation is seen in the final two verses, 8–9, when the psalmist asks God to save the people and be their shepherd.

Finally, the psalmist often uses two different kinds of expression for giving thanks. One involves the word *bless*. The psalmist blesses the Lord, meaning that the psalmist is giving thanks to God. The other is that the psalmist vows to make an offering, a thank offering, as a way of saying thanks to God (Miller, 1994, 179–181, 194–201).

Vowing to Praise

The vow of praise may include thanks, but this form of praising God also goes beyond thanks, because it involves enthusiastically proclaiming such things as appreciation, respect, and admiration for God. In addition, praise may address everything from creation to different positive experiences associated with God. Miller calls praise a form of prayer that "can praise God for very specific moments and deeds of help, but it can also, more expansively, praise God for the creation and for all sorts of ways that God has shown steadfast love and manifested glory" (1994, 214).

You can see these differences when you compare songs of thanksgiving with hymns of praise. These hymns are psalms entirely about praise. As we have seen, songs of thanksgiving express gratitude for a specific divine act bringing deliverance. The main difference in a hymn of praise is that it is a more general expression, not tied to any particular act of God. "The psalmist expresses praise in more general terms, extolling the God whose name is majestic in heaven and earth, whose sovereign might rules human history" (Anderson, 2000, 101). One of the best known hymns of praise is Psalm 100:

> Make a joyful noise to the LORD, all the earth.
>> Worship the LORD with gladness;
>> come into his presence with singing.
> Know that the LORD is God.
>> It is he that made us, and we are his;
>> We are his people, and the sheep of his pasture.
> Enter his gates with thanksgiving,
>> and his courts with praise.
>> Give thanks to him, bless his name.

Praise in lament psalms is not different from praise in hymns of praise. Both expand beyond thanks. Yet the vow of praise in the lament psalms still is expressed in anticipation of God's future deliverance. Psalm 69:30–36, a vow of praise and thanksgiving, is a good example showing how praise can branch beyond thanks even in lament psalms, while retaining a future orientation:

> I will praise the name of God with a song;
>   I will magnify him with thanksgiving.
> This will please the LORD more than an ox
>   or a bull with horns and hoofs.
> Let the oppressed see it and be glad;
>   you who seek God, let your hearts revive.
> For the LORD hears the needy,
>   and does not despise his own that are in bonds.
> Let heaven and earth praise him,
>   the seas and everything that moves in them.
> For God will save Zion
>   and rebuild the cities of Judah;
> and his servants shall live there and possess it;
>   the children of his servants shall inherit it,
>   and those who love his name shall live in it.

Toward Community

Recall from chapter seven that in ancient Israelite worship, the worship leader may have spoken an oracle of salvation, to which the congregation responded with praise and thanks. In this part of the liturgy, the petitioner who sought God's help was making a vow in the midst of the congregation. In the context of worship, the vow of praise and thanksgiving was not private, but communal. According to Miller, "The loneliness and abandonment that are often the symptoms, if not the manifestations, of the distress are overcome as the suppliant stands in the midst of the whole community." This is in accord with one important purpose of individual prayers for help, restoring the person to community: "Here we can see the appropriateness of the claim that one of the purposes of the individual prayers for help—and whatever ritual accompanied them—was the restoration of the afflicted individual to full participation and acceptance in the community." Indeed, Miller goes on to say that one of the main effects of thanks and praise is creation of community: "The creation of community is one of the primary effects of praise and thanksgiving" (1994, 131).

Disclosing a World

If praise and thanksgiving relates and restores people to community, these two ways of praising God also disclose the kind of world in which the community resides. Praise and thanks, insists Miller, presume that God is creator of the world. Otherwise, praising God would make no sense. Praise, writes Miller, "assumes and even evokes...a world where impossible things become possible, where things too difficult become the order of the day." The joy of praising God is evoked by, and evokes, living in a world in which God truly acts (1994, 223–24).

The Vow of Praise and Thanksgiving of Contemporary Psalmists of Lament

Contemporary psalmists of lament conclude their psalm with a vow of praise and thanksgiving, made in the assurance that God has heard their prayer and will act. This contemporary psalm of lament reflects reconnection with community and contains a view of the world as God's creation. The sixth mourning process provides content informing of the vow. Reinvesting gives the psalmist something about which to be thankful and a reason to offer praise. This fits quite well with the future orientation of the vow of praise and thanksgiving, because the desired results of the reinvesting may not be realized immediately. Some desired results take years to materialize. For instance, a mourner who returns to school in pursuit of a new career may have to wait several years for the result.

Some reinvestments yield desired results bringing personal satisfaction primarily, while other reinvestments are meant to yield results that are rewarding for other individuals or the community. Contemporary psalmists of lament have great flexibility and a variety of possibilities when they offer their praise and thanks to God. Some contemporary vows may focus more on thanks than praise, while others may be the opposite.

Vowing to Give Thanks

Several years ago, a famous sports figure lost his wife to cancer. For two years following her death, he hardly could play his sport and remained deeply immersed in grief and mourning. Then, he was introduced to a woman with whom he developed a new relationship. After a time, they married and now have a family. In a television interview, he discussed his unending love for his deceased wife and his sense of her continuing presence. Remarkably, he conveyed his belief, or rather his certainty, that his deceased wife approves of his present wife and blesses their marriage. His present wife expressed sharing this belief in the deceased wife's approval.

Seen in terms of the sixth mourning process, the husband has transferred emotional energy previously invested in his deceased wife and is redirecting it toward a new marriage and family. At the same time, he continues investing energy in his ongoing relationship with his deceased wife. His reinvestment is in the service of healthy living in the present, and it yields the rewards that marriage and family bring.

Several years have passed since he first met his present wife. His reinvestment has paid off, and he is living fruitfully in the new world. He could pray a full-blown song of thanksgiving, looking back on how God helped and giving thanks for it. Likewise, he could pray a hymn of praise, expressing appreciation and respect for God. However, when he was introduced to his present wife, and as mutual interest was kindled, and even when the marriage was brand new, his reinvestment was fresh and new, and many of the desired results were still in the future. For instance, the relationship still needed to mature, and they did not have children yet. At this early point in the relationship, he still would be praying as a psalmist of lament.

If, as a contemporary psalmist of lament, the mourner were to make an explicit vow of praise and thanks it might be oriented primarily toward thanks, and it could go something like this:

> *Thank you, Lord, for hearing my prayer for help*
> *during the darkness of the past few years;*
> *for I can walk again in the light of love.*
> *Thank you, Lord, for my wife,*
> *and the opportunity for us to make a new life together.*
> *I promise you that I will be grateful to you always*
> *for the unfolding of our marriage relationship during the*
> *   years ahead,*
> *and I will share my admiration for you to all who will listen.*

Vowing to Praise God

In a recent movie *The Visitor*, a college professor has become a widower. We never know how his wife died or how long ago she died. We do find out that she was a musician who played the piano. The opening scene finds the professor taking a piano lesson. Internalizing his wife's musical talent seems to be the main way he is attempting to continue relating to her in the present, but he is not successful at learning to play. As the piano teacher leaves his house after a lesson, she inquires about buying the piano if he ever decides to sell it. He just looks at her.

At work, he has lost all interest, teaching his classes like a robot and showing no concern for students. During the semester something happens that changes the course of his life. He has allowed his name to be used on an academic paper mostly written by a younger colleague, and this colleague is to present it at a conference in New York City, not far from the college. At the last minute, the colleague is not able to attend the conference, so the professor is forced to present the paper instead. He attends the conference, which lasts for several days, and presents the paper. It goes fine, but the real action is happening outside the conference.

When the professor arrives in the city for the conference, he stays at an apartment he has owned for many years, a kind of home away from home. He unlocks the door, enters the apartment, and receives a real shock. A young couple is living there, having rented it from an unscrupulous apartment manager. They leave, but he rushes into the street, inviting them to stay with him until they find a new place to live, and they accept. The professor has begun an odyssey of reinvestment.

The young woman is from Africa, and the young man has fled from Syria, because his father had written against the government. They both are illegal immigrants. The young man is a talented musician who plays a kind of drum struck with the hands, not drumsticks. Gradually, the young man and the professor become friends, as the professor delays returning to work after the conference and then later travels back and forth between his work and the city apartment. He begins accompanying the young man to the park where he plays music with others and to his job playing with a jazz band in a nightclub. Finally, the professor even begins learning how to play the drum, as a new spark of life becomes visible in his face and demeanor.

Then tragedy strikes. The young man is arrested and taken to a detention center where he remains for weeks on end. A new character now comes on the scene, the mother of the young man. She has come to New York to check on her son who has not been answering his phone. She meets the young woman for the first time and discovers that her son has been arrested. The professor helps them and visits the young man regularly. Sadly, however, he is deported, sent back to Syria where he will be in danger. During this period of time, the professor and the mother have become friends and begun caring for each other. But this relationship, too, is destined to end. After her son is deported, she decides she must return to Syria to help her son as she is able, but the young woman stays in New York City.

The professor's reinvestment began with a snap judgment to let the young couple stay in his apartment temporarily, and gradually he began redirecting his emotional energy toward new relationships in the present. At the same time, he finally found a way to maintain a connection with his deceased wife in the present through music, but his playing also represented something more. He was not a pianist, but he was a drummer, which brings us to the final scene and his implicit vow of praise.

The professor takes a leave of absence from teaching, and the movie ends with him back in New York City, stepping out of a subway car carrying his drum. He sits down on the terminal and begins to play, experiencing new life as if resurrected from the dead, a new life that is just beginning. What is more, playing the drum in the subway is his vow of praise. Seen as a contemporary psalmist of lament, the professor's vow of praise could be:

> *I was lost, and now I am found, God.*
> *I will find the best way I know to express*
> *my respect, admiration, and appreciation for you.*
> *I know that my drum playing is not much,*
> *but every beat will be my hymn of praise to you*
> *in the community for all to hear.*

Beyond Reinvesting

Once a contemporary psalmist of lament reaches the part of the psalm involving the vow of praise and thanksgiving, reconnection with community has occurred and a vision of a world seen as God's creation has formed or been reaffirmed. This is a world in which God acts, bringing deliverance to the person or group needing help, though this help may be in the future. God's action in the world may not be seen as it was before the death or during the difficult periods of grief and mourning. An assumption about God acting helpfully in the world had possibly been shattered. The vow of praise and thanksgiving indicates that such a shattered assumption has been replaced with a more realistic interpretation of God acting in the world.

Living in this world for the long term means living with an attitude of praise and thanks. Reinvestments yield rewards of personal satisfaction, but they also benefit others. The professor was a melancholy figure who appeared to be rather uncompassionate at the beginning of *The Visitor*. As he became increasingly involved with the illegal immigrants, his compassion emerged, or reemerged. He now had the possibility of living as a compassionate and caring person, like he perhaps had done years ago as a teacher. Contemporary psalmists of lament who reach the point of expressing a vow of praise and thanksgiving have the opportunity to embrace living as part of God's creation, in which gratitude toward God and respect for God become the foundation for treating others with gratitude and respect, reflected in compassion and caring.

Implications for the Ministry of Lament

Those who practice the ministry of lament stand with the bereaved during difficult times. Yet the sixth mourning process and the final part of the lament psalms show that this caring ministry also is celebratory. Pastors and church members support the efforts of contemporary psalmists of lament to live in the new world in a healthy manner as they reinvest in relationships and activities.

This positive support takes wisdom. Pastors or church members may not see that a particular reinvestment actually will yield the result desired. Perhaps it is a false start, and the mourner must try again. Contemporary psalmists of lament need the freedom to experiment with reinvestment, requiring those who care to withhold judgment. A pastor or group of church members may expect the mourner to resume exactly the same relationships and behaviors engaged in before the death. Instead, the mourner may need to go in a whole new direction that does not seem practical on the surface. The professor's involvement with the illegal immigrants, combined with his neglect of teaching, seems impractical viewed from a distance. Yet in reality his reinvestments were healthy and brought new life. The ministry of lament requires openness to change on the part of contemporary psalmists of lament.

Finally, a contemporary psalmist of lament living anew in praise and thanksgiving has the opportunity to join those who practice the ministry of lament, putting compassion and care to work in the service of caring for others who grieve. One Sunday after worship, a pastor was getting into her car to drive home, when she saw two church members getting into a car, as if to go out for lunch. One of the women had been a widow for six weeks. The other woman had been a widow for several years. Previously, these two women had not been friendly with each other, but now the longtime widow was practicing the ministry of lament with a new mourner.

Their lunch together was not an official counseling conversation with the pastor or an assigned visit by a trained lay caregiver. These other things may happen at different times, and they are part of the overall ministry of lament. But they are no more valuable than the unofficial care practiced at lunch that day. One of the most overlooked and neglected aspects of caring ministry in the church is the unofficial care practiced by lay individuals and groups in congregations. In the ministry of lament, contemporary psalmists of lament become part of the community that cares for bereaved people.

Becoming Witnesses: A Final Conclusion

At the end of chapter one, I wrote that the rest of the book would be concerned with spirituality and grief in the service of contributing to caring ministry with the bereaved, which I have called the ministry of lament. Through the dialogue between mourning and the lament psalms, I have characterized those who are rewriting their bereaved life story as contemporary psalmists of lament. This has been a way to discuss the spiritual rewriting taking place in relation to the mourning processes.

Pastors and congregations who practice the ministry of lament have much to learn from contemporary psalmists of lament, because these psalmists know what it is like to grow in relationship to God during the course of rewriting a bereaved life story. As psalmists, they become poets who cry out to God for help in prayer. They experience complaint, bringing the awfulness of their suffering to light, facing their alienation from God, and wrestling with the perennial human questions about suffering. They also reach the point of confessing trust in God's reliability, not by avoiding complaint but by facing it. They make specific petitions for help, and they experience assurance that God hears their prayer and will act. They know what it means to be grateful to God in the aftermath of all that has happened, and they genuinely respect, admire, and appreciate God, which we see in their praise.

Contemporary psalmists of lament become witnesses to the possibility of sustaining a relationship with the God from whom we do not have to hide anything, even our worst thoughts and feelings. God is the one with whom we can relate in significantly different ways during experiences of tremendous upheaval and change. God is the one who assures us that we are heard, that we do not have to be afraid, and that the future holds the promise of deliverance. Such witnesses can contribute powerfully to the church's understanding of God in relation to the human family during times of sorrow and suffering that bereavement brings. Ultimately, we all share in this witness, because we all become psalmists of lament during the course of living as part of God's creation.

References

Anderson, Bernhard W., with Steven Bishop (2000). *Out of the Depths: The Psalms Speak For Us Today* (3d ed., revised and expanded). Louisville: Westminster John Knox Press.

Attig, Thomas (1996). *How We Grieve: Relearning the World*. New York: Oxford University Press.

_____ (2000). *The Heart of Grief: Death and the Search for Lasting Love*. New York: Oxford University Press.

Berry, Wendell (2000). *Jayber Crow*. New York: Counterpoint.

Bidwell, Duane R. (2005). "We Will Be Changed: Resurrection and Grief." In *Reflections on Grief and Spiritual Growth*, edited by A. J. Weaver and H. W. Stone, 40–51. Nashville: Abingdon Press.

Brown, William P. (2002). *Seeing the Psalms: A Theology of Metaphor*. Louisville: Westminster John Knox Press.

Brueggemann, Walter (1984). *The Message of the Psalms: A Theological Commentary*. Minneapolis: Augsburg.

_____ (1995). *Psalms and the Life of Faith*, edited by P. D. Miller. Minneapolis: Fortress Press.

Buechner, Frederick (1991). *Telling Secrets*. San Francisco: HarperSanFrancisco.

Capps, Donald (1981). *Biblical Approaches to Pastoral Counseling*. Philadelphia: The Westminster Press.

Cole, Allan Hugh, Jr. (2008). *Good Mourning: Getting Through Your Grief*. Louisville: Westminster John Knox Press.

Crenshaw, James L. (2001). *The Psalms: An Introduction*. Grand Rapids: William B. Eerdmans Publishing Company.

deClaissé-Walford, Nancy L. (2004). *Introduction to the Psalms: A Song from Ancient Israel*. St. Louis: Chalice Press.

Didion, Joan (2007). *The Year of Magical Thinking*. New York: Vintage Books.

Doehring, Carrie (2006). *The Practice of Pastoral Care: A Postmodern Approach*. Louisville: Westminster John Knox Press.

Duff, Nancy J. (2005). "Recovering Lamentation as a Practice in the Church." In *Lament: Reclaiming Practices in Pulpit, Pew, and Public Square*, edited by S. A. Brown and P. D. Miller, 3–14. Louisville: Westminster John Knox Press.

Fowler, Gene (2004). *Caring Through the Funeral: A Pastor's Guide.* St. Louis: Chalice Press.

Freud, Sigmund (1957). "Mourning and Melancholia." In *The Standard Edition of the Complete Psychological Works of Sigmund Freud,* vol. 14, edited and translated by J. Strachey. London: Hogarth (original work published 1915).

Gunkel, Hermann (1967). *The Psalms: A Form-Critical Introduction.* Introduction by James Muilenburg. Translated by Thomas M. Horner. Philadelphia: Fortress Press.

Irion, Paul E. (1954). *The Funeral and the Mourners: Pastoral Care of the Bereaved.* Nashville: Abingdon Press.

Janoff-Bulman, Ronnie (1992). *Shattered Assumptions: Towards a New Psychology of Trauma.* New York: The Free Press.

Kauffman, Jeffrey (2002). "Safety and the Assumptive World: A Theory of Traumatic Loss." In *Loss of the Assumptive World: A Theory of Traumatic Loss,* edited by J. Kauffman, 205–211. New York: Brunner-Routledge.

Klass, Dennis (2001). "The Inner Representation of the Dead Child in the Psychic and Social Narratives of Bereaved Parents." In *Meaning Reconstruction & the Experience of Loss,* edited by R. A. Neimeyer, 77–94. Washington, D.C.: American Psychological Association.

Kübler-Ross, Elisabeth (1969). *On Death and Dying.* New York: MacMillan.

Lamott, Anne (1999). *Traveling Mercies: Some Thoughts on Faith.* New York: Anchor.

Lindemann, Erich (1979). *Beyond Grief: Studies in Crisis Intervention.* Introduction by Bertram S. Brown. London: Jason Aronson, Inc. First printed as Lindemann, Erich (1944). "Symptomatology and Management of Acute Grief." *American Journal of Psychiatry,* 101, 141–148.

Mays, James Luther. (2006). *Preaching and Teaching the Psalms,* edited by P. D. Miller and G. M. Tucker. Louisville: Westminster John Knox Press.

McCann, J. Clinton, Jr. (1992). "The Psalms as Instruction." *Interpretation: A Journal of Bible and Theology* 46, no. 2: 117–128.

———— (1993). *A Theological Introduction to the Book of Psalms: The Psalms as Torah.* Nashville: Abingdon Press.

Miller, Patrick D. (1994). *They Cried to the Lord: The Form and Theology of Biblical Prayer.* Minneapolis: Fortress Press.

Neimeyer, Robert A., ed. (2001). *Meaning Reconstruction & the Experience of Loss*. Washington, D.C.: American Psychological Association.

Neimeyer, Robert A. (2001). "Meaning Reconstruction and Loss." In *Meaning Reconstruction & the Experience of Loss*, edited by R. A. Neimeyer, 1–9. Washington, D.C.: American Psychological Association.

_____ (2001). "The Language of Loss: Grief Therapy as a Process of Meaning Reconstruction." In *Meaning Reconstruction & the Experience of Loss*, edited by R. A. Neimeyer, 261–292. Washington, D.C.: American Psychological Association.

Neimeyer, Robert A., et al., (2002). "The Meaning of Your Absence: Traumatic Loss and Narrative Reconstruction." In *Loss of the Assumptive World: A Theory of Traumatic Loss*, edited by J. Kauffman, 31–47. New York: Brunner-Routledge.

Oxford English Dictionary, 2d ed. (1989). Oxford: Clarendon Press.

Patton, John (1993). *Pastoral Care in Context: An Introduction to Pastoral Care*. Louisville: Westminster/John Knox Press.

Rando, Therese A. (1993). *Treatment of Complicated Mourning*. Champaign, Ill.: Research Press.

Shneidman, Edwin (1993). *Suicide as Psychache: A Clinical Approach to Self-Destructive Behavior*. London: Jason Aronson Inc.

Smith, Harold Ivan (2001). *When Your People Are Grieving: Leading in Times of Loss*. Kansas City, Mo.: Beacon Hill Press of Kansas City.

Switzer, David (1974). *The Minister as Crisis Counselor*. Nashville: Abingdon Press.

_____ (2000). *Pastoral Care Emergencies*. Minneapolis: Fortress Press.

Weaver, Andrew J., and Howard W. Stone (2005). *Reflections on Grief and Spiritual Growth*. Nashville: Abingdon Press.

Weems, Ann (1995). *Psalms of Lament*. Foreword by Walter Brueggemann. Louisville: Westminster John Knox Press.

Westermann, Claus (1965). *The Praise of God in the Psalms*. Translated by Keith R. Crim. Richmond, Va.: John Knox Press.

Wuthnow, Robert (2007). *After the Baby Boomers: How Twenty-and-Thirty-Somethings are Shaping the Future of American Religion*. Princeton: Princeton University Press.

LaVergne, TN USA
09 February 2011
215915LV00005B/74/P